# Professional Learning Redefined

*To Chip, Church, Jake, and Reid—you all have both inspired and grounded me throughout this process. I hope I make you proud! To Mimi and Ma—I am happy to follow in your footsteps!*

—Isabel

*To J & A, you are always my inspiration and my support.*

—Marisa

# Professional Learning Redefined

## An Evidence-Based Guide

Isabel Sawyer

Marisa Ramirez Stukey

*Foreword by Diane Sweeney*

A Joint Publication

FOR INFORMATION:

Corwin

A SAGE Company

2455 Teller Road

Thousand Oaks, California 91320

(800) 233-9936

www.corwin.com

SAGE Publications Ltd.

1 Oliver's Yard

55 City Road

London EC1Y 1SP

United Kingdom

SAGE Publications India Pvt. Ltd.

B 1/I 1 Mohan Cooperative Industrial Area

Mathura Road, New Delhi 110 044

India

SAGE Publications Asia-Pacific Pte. Ltd.

18 Cross Street #10-10/11/12

China Square Central

Singapore 048423

Printed in the United States of America

Library of Congress Cataloging-in-Publication Data

Names: Sawyer, Isabel, author. | Stukey, Marisa Ramirez, author.

Title: Professional learning redefined : an evidence-based guide / Isabel Sawyer, Marisa Ramirez Stukey ; foreword by Diane Sweeney.

Description: Thousand Oaks, California : Corwin, [2019] | Includes bibliographical references and index.

Identifiers: LCCN 2018047974 | ISBN 9781544336756 (pbk. : acid-free paper)

Subjects: LCSH: Teachers–In-service training–United States. | Teachers–Professional relationships–United States. | Professional learning communities–United States.

Classification: LCC LB1731 .S29 2019 | DDC 370.71/10973–dc23 LC record available at https://lccn.loc.gov/2018047974

This book is printed on acid-free paper.

Program Director and Publisher:  Dan Alpert

Content Development Editor:  Lucas Schleicher

Senior Editorial Assistant:  Mia Rodriguez

Project Editor:  Amy Schroller

Copy Editor:  Michelle Ponce

Typesetter:  Cenveo

Proofreader:  Laura Webb

Indexer:  Maria Sosnowski

Cover Designer:  Candice Harmon

Marketing Manager:  Sharon Pendergast

SUSTAINABLE FORESTRY INITIATIVE

Certified Chain of Custody
Promoting Sustainable Forestry
www.sfiprogram.org
SFI-01268

SFI label applies to text stock

19 20 21 22 23 10 9 8 7 6 5 4 3 2 1

# Contents

Visit the companion website at
resources.corwin.com/ProfessionalLearningRedefined
for downloadable resources.

# Tool Index

## CHAPTER 2: LEARNING WITHIN CONTENT

| | |
|---|---|
| Curricular Resource Planning Tool | A guide for planning professional learning alongside curricular resources—helpful in considering whether or not you can use your curricular tool for ongoing support |

## CHAPTER 3: ELEMENTS OF LEARNING

| | |
|---|---|
| Effective Elements of Professional Learning | Intended to help consider the four elements (content, coherence, duration, and collaboration) but not intended to be used as a "checklist" |

## CHAPTER 4: LEARNING STRUCTURES

| | |
|---|---|
| Four Corners | Teambuilder |
| Compass Points | Teambuilder |
| Norm Setting | Guidelines for initial norm setting with teams |
| Chalk Talk | Supports collaboration and active learning through brainstorming content around a particular topic—allows the participants to share their thinking through a silent written brainstorming session |
| Quote Cards | Aids in discussing big instructional ideas and is a vehicle for offering some conceptual inputs |
| Philosophical Chairs | Supports the processing of different opinions |
| Consultancy Protocol | Resource to ground the conversation in daily work and give teachers the chance to share their thinking around problems they are facing |
| Final Word | Text rendering protocol that offers the chance for learners to agree with or argue with one another safely about important instructional ideas and research in their reading |
| Archetypal Spaces for Learning | Possible structure for a book study or deeper exploration of a topic |
| Planning Guide for Twitter Chats | Ideas to think about when organizing a Twitter Chat |

## CHAPTER 5: LEAD LEARNER

| | |
|---|---|
| **Preparing for and Debriefing a Demonstration Lesson** | Guide for facilitating a demonstration lesson—support for considering the direction to take the learning, deciding where to probe further, and how to redirect thinking |
| **PDSA Cycle** | Framework to consider the plan of action in a clear, coherent, and action-focused manner. |
| **Questions to Ask While Planning** | Questions that will be useful when planning for any work you might support with learning teams, each linked to the research-based characteristic discussed earlier in the book |

## CHAPTER 6: CONNECTING THE LEARNING

| | |
|---|---|
| **Planning the Change Process** | Support thinking around the change process in a district |
| **Planning for Sustained Professional Learning** | Comprehensive planning document |

# Foreword

The power of high quality professional learning is not to be underestimated. It provides the opportunity to collaborate and reflect on teaching practice, the curriculum, and student performance. I suspect that if you picked up this book, you agree with this premise.

What becomes tricky is designing and delivering professional learning in a way that moves student learning and teacher practice forward. This task often falls on school and district leaders who are juggling many responsibilities. How many of us have sat at our desks and wondered, "What are we going to do in our [fill in the blank] meeting next week?" Or, "How am I going to make the meeting relevant, engaging, and focused on student learning so that teachers don't feel like it was a waste of time?" The pressure is real.

In *Professional Learning Redefined*, Sawyer and Stukey present a conceptual design for professional learning that is rooted in the research. This includes making the case that effective professional learning impacts student and teacher outcomes. They argue that duration and evaluation of impact are essential, as is building content knowledge and coherence for teachers. Together, these elements create a vision for professional learning that is student-centered and outcomes-based.

Having spent decades as a practioner, author, and coach, I have learned the importance of putting student learning front and center. This led me to develop a model for instructional coaching known as Student-Centered Coaching—an approach that operates under the same conceptual framework as what is offered here. For example, we provide duration through the use of coaching cycles. We ensure student outcomes through goal setting that is standards-based. We monitor and evaluate student learning through the development of learning targets. And we develop instructional and content knowledge through co-planning and co-teaching sessions. These practices are echoed in what Sawyer and Stukey offer as qualities of effective professional learning.

I've often struggled to find a resource that presents the research for adult learning in a way that is practical and actionable. I'd search for protocols online, read about adult learning in a book, and find facilitation strategies someplace else.

How inefficient is that? *Professional Learning Redefined* puts everything one needs to engage adult learners in one place. It explores not only the research on effective professional learning but also the skills, strategies, and tools that are required to make it happen. This includes a look at theories of adult learning, the key components of high quality professional learning, collaborative structures, protocols, and characteristics for effective facilitation. When sitting down to plan professional learning, this will now be my "go-to" resource. It is organized, accessible, and rich with tools that any reader can use tomorrow. Some of my favorite are the protocols and planning documents.

We must constantly ask ourselves, "Are the students at the center of this conversation?" If not, then our professional learning structures are failing to serve us.

We all want teachers to feel inspired and supported, yet executing on this demands a vast amount of knowledge, skills, and strategies. Reading this book provides just that.

—**Diane Sweeney**
Author of *Leading Student-Centered Coaching* (2018), and
Creator of Diane Sweeney Consulting

# Preface

From our first conversation about crafting this book, we realized it was a desire each of us had had for a long time. We both spend much of our professional lives helping districts think about changing instructional practices—and had searched for a book that would support our work in the professional learning arena. To our surprise, we could not find one resource that would help us think about the big picture. How do we systematically change practice, from individual classrooms to entire districts? We had some old favorite books and articles that we each loved and pulled out on a regular basis to guide our practice; however, there wasn't one resource that we felt met all of our needs as we supported teachers and districts to change and grow. We recognized that real learning is messy, and there is not a single correct answer in every situation. Yet, still we struggled to find answers to the questions we had, and now, we plan on using this book as a resource for some of our most challenging dilemmas.

The principles of professional learning and development outlined in this book are grounded in the ever-increasing body of research on professional development and professional learning. We know that one-and-done workshops aren't the answer. Our hope is to offer some thinking on the big picture—how we actually make sense of the research that is available to us on professional learning and use that research to inform the learning we engage in, from coaching sessions, to PLC conversations, to workshops, to multiyear professional learning plans.

## OUTLINE OF THE BOOK

At the heart, this text is about leading learning and is written for educators who support teachers—oftentimes, these people are coaches, principals, reading specialists, or district leaders. Whatever your role, each chapter in this book is designed to support your thinking about the research-based practices of professional learning and translate that research into action.

Chapter 1 will focus on current policy and policy changes over the last ten years related to professional learning. When we understand the context, we are better able to support deep learning and change. Chapter 1 also explores the differences between professional learning and professional development and the important role of adult learners. Additionally, this chapter reviews the current research on the elements and mechanisms of powerful professional learning.

Chapter 2 delves into the role of content knowledge in supporting teacher professional learning. It is clear that professional learning about general classroom practices does not lead to sustained teacher change and student achievement. While the following chapter will dig deeper into the professional learning strategies themselves, this chapter will consider how we embed the content into the learning experiences for educators. We explore deeply the role of curriculum as a vehicle and support for content-based professional learning.

Chapter 3 explains the researched-based elements of professional learning. There is a well-researched set of characteristics that comprise quality professional learning experiences. We will discuss each individually and give examples of how those characteristics come to life. We will also begin to discuss the ways in which these characteristics overlap and support one another in deepening teacher learning.

Chapter 4 helps frame what the research suggests about the professional learning experiences that educators engage in and how they make an impact on changes in practice. This chapter focuses on the mechanisms (such as PLCs and coaching) for bringing the features described in the previous chapters to life. We describe what kinds of activities support and use these characteristics and offer questions to use as a guide when planning.

Chapter 5 will focus on the facilitator. The role of the facilitator of professional learning is often a neglected aspect of professional learning. Research suggests that many endeavors hinge on the quality and knowledge of the facilitator leading the learning (Borko, 2004). In this chapter, we'll explore how the facilitator uses the content and the context to plan for the learning to take place. We will also explore the stance of the facilitator and how that has an impact on the professional learning itself and also how the facilitator's stance is a model for the teaching stance.

Chapter 6 makes the case for the ways the characteristics, mechanisms, and the facilitator come together and interact. A framework is used to show the interconnected nature of the work and how the elements interact. It brings to life the way in which we consider our audience, task, and purpose. An implementation framework will be shared illustrating how the many features and mechanisms coexist and complement each other and can be used for planning a multiyear implementation.

All of the tools, charts, and guides referenced in the book are housed in the appendix. This was designed to support your own planning and is intended for you to use as blackline masters. Our goal was to truly make this a book a go-to for all your planning needs.

## HOW TO USE THIS BOOK

You might consider reading this book in order. The chapters were designed to build on each other and give context to designing a professional learning system. Alternatively, you may want to dive right into understanding a particular aspect of professional learning. We might suggest you start by looking at reflection questions at the end of each chapter. They will help you think about the possible answers you could be searching for and whether or not they can be found in the chapter you chose. The chapters can be read when you most need them.

Our hope is that you will use the quotes, stories, and protocols that we have shared in your own work. We've shared vignettes from our own experience, from our colleagues' experience, as well as some we created to illustrate the interconnectivity and power of strong professional learning. We hope that you will learn facilitative techniques that support powerful professional learning for teachers while also mirroring the techniques teachers will use with students. We will share tools that support planning for active professional learning to support these shifts in instruction—both at the school and district level. Finally, we will help you create a plan for supporting shifts in professional learning that lead to shifts in instruction. Let's get started!

# Acknowledgments

First and foremost, thank you to all of the educators that we have worked with, coached and been mentored by—many of whom inspired vignettes (and even helped write some of them). Your insights and partnership in learning have proven invaluable to us.

We are also grateful to many of the amazing districts that have informed our thinking—Albemarle, Charlotte-Mecklenburg, St. Johns County, Virginia Beach, and P. K. Yonge Developmental Research School at the University of Florida. Our work with you has taught us so much.

Thank you to the amazing and collaborative teams with whom we have worked. We are forever in debt to the regional directors at the Center for the Collaborative Classroom for their support and feedback. We are especially appreciative of our own teams in the Mid-Atlantic and South! Thanks for allowing us the time and space to make this book a reality.

Speaking of our colleagues at the Center for the Collaborative Classroom, we are forever in debt to Kelly Stuart, our fearless leader—without her, this book would not have been written. We are so grateful for your belief in us, willingness to support us, and constant cheerleading. We love you! Another special thanks to Sue Wilder for helping us think through and push back. As always, your encouragement that we CAN do this has been such an inspiration. And finally, Peter Brunn, you blazed a trail, and we're thankful for you being the first!

Thank you to Keri Bartholomew for helping us share an important story. Thank you to Claire Riddell for helping our voices to read more seamlessly and for proving the critical feedback that we needed. We so appreciate you.

Thank you to our Publisher, Dan Alpert. Your belief that our voices were welcome was the exact push we needed to get started. Thank you to Mia and Lucas, our Senior Editorial Assistant and Content Development Editor, for their patience and expertise.

Finally, to our families, we are beyond grateful to you.

## Publisher's Acknowledgments

Corwin gratefully acknowledges the contributions of the following reviewers:

Marine Avagyan
Director of Curriculum and Instruction
Saugus Union School District
Santa Clarita, CA

Claudia A. Danna
Adjunct Professor
Sacred Heart University
Griswold, CT

Dara Feldman
Educational Consultant
The Heart of Education, LLC
Kensington, MD

Jacie Maslyk
Assistant Superintendent
Hopewell Area School District
Beaver County, PA

Ronda J. Mitchell
Assistant Professor
University of Illinois at Springfield
Springfield, IL

Melissa Nixon
Director of Title I
Guilford County Schools
Greensboro, NC

Lena Marie Rockwood
Assistant Principal
Revere High School
Revere, MA

# About the Authors

Isabel Sawyer          Marisa Ramirez Stukey

**Isabel Sawyer** and **Marisa Ramirez Stukey** are both regional directors at the Center for the Collaborative Classroom, a nonprofit organization devoted to the academic, social, and ethical development of children. Much of what you will read in their book is due to their experiences at Collaborative Classroom and as public school educators and university professors. They owe a great deal of debt to their colleagues, with whom and from whom they have learned. They have both been blessed to have incredible teams to learn from both at Collaborative Classroom and in their public school districts.

Isabel is a long time Virginia educator. She grew up as an educator working in Albemarle County schools at the foothills of the Blue Ridge Mountains in Virginia. She trained early on in her career as a Reading Recovery teacher. This intensive training transformed the way she thought about teaching and learning. She then completed her doctorate in Curriculum and Instruction at the University of Virginia. Before coming to the Center for the Collaborative Classroom, Isabel served as a lead instructional coach in Albemarle County schools, supporting the work of instructional coaches and leadership teams. She continues to serve as an adjunct instructor at the University of Virginia, teaching teachers who are working on their masters' degrees in reading education.

Marisa knew she was going to be a teacher from her earliest days of rounding up the neighborhood kids and forcing them to endure her "reading" lessons in the backyard. She has vivid memories of her first-grade teacher giving her an old teacher's edition of a reading basal! Marisa has served as a primary teacher, university instructor, curriculum coordinator, and administrator at both the school and district levels. She completed her doctorate in Curriculum, Teaching, and Teacher Education at the University of Florida where the emphasis was on literacy and teacher professional learning.

They have a strong partnership—due to their differences. Marisa has a much more polished and thoughtful writing style; Isabel is more comfortable writing when she allows her voice to shine. These strengths form a particularly nice union when merged together—they hope readers find their perspectives and writing style accessible.

Now, who are you? Take a moment and reflect on your professional role and your goals for reading this book. Perhaps you are a school-based coach who is tasked with designing professional learning experiences for your school? Perhaps you are a district literacy specialist tasked with supporting teachers in implementing a new curriculum? Perhaps you are an assistant principal who is tasked with supervising the quality of instruction in your school and supporting teachers in making changes in their practice? Whatever your official role, you all have a stake in teacher professional learning and student achievement.

# CHAPTER 1

# Learning in the Teaching Profession

As a young teacher, Kimrey felt lost and alone. Kimrey's first-grade classroom was next to her mentor teacher's room, and she tried to connect daily with her mentor, Paula, because she knew she needed help. Every morning when she entered Paula's classroom, she was struck by a poster that was on the wall of Paula's room. It was a black and white picture of Haim Ginott with the following quote printed on it: "I've come to a frightening conclusion that I am the decisive element in the classroom. It's my personal approach that creates the climate. It's my daily mood that makes the weather. As a teacher, I possess a tremendous power to make a child's life miserable or joyous. I can be a tool of torture or an instrument of inspiration. I can humiliate or heal. In all situations, it is my response that decides whether a crisis will be escalated or de-escalated and a child humanized or dehumanized."

Haim Ginott's quote gave Kimrey nightmares. She knew she was often a "tool of torture" for her students, yet she had no idea how to make things better in her classroom. Her routines weren't clear or consistent, and her students misbehaved. Not only that, she had no idea how to plan for an effective guided reading lesson, and her students were not learning to read. Kimrey attended her district's beginning of the year sessions designed to help new teachers learn more about the different levels of engagement but never figured out how this information connected with her six-year-olds, much less teaching phonics. She participated in the state's novice teacher assistance program and used a read aloud lesson during her observation that she had perfected and practiced several times in order to get a positive review from her evaluator. Finally, at the end of her first year, Kimrey decided to leave the teaching field. Her principal was relieved as her students had the lowest test scores in first grade.

This vignette is not unusual. We've all known a teacher like Kimrey or someone similar. While a first year teacher has specific needs, all teachers need a system of support and continued learning. When we look at that system for Kimrey, it was weak at best. She was not offered the professional learning opportunities that she needed in order to be successful. The content was not focused, there was no intentional thread of learning throughout her first year, and she was not given the kind of thoughtful support that would have supported her learning.

*Change is what teachers do and think. It's as simple and as complex as that.*

—Fullan, 1982, p. 107

In the last twenty years, teacher quality and professional development have become pressing issues in our nation. Many reform efforts have promoted professional development as a viable path for increased school success and student achievement. In the early 2000s, the No Child Left Behind Act (U.S. Congress, 2001) required states to provide access to "high quality" professional development that builds teachers' subject-area knowledge, teaching skills, and technological skills. In 2004, The Teaching Commission published a call to action, *Teaching at Risk: A Call to Action* (McGowan, 2004). They suggested that "helping our teachers succeed and enabling our children to learn is an investment in human potential" (p. 11). The report called for enticing and keeping the most capable teachers. They also offered specific policy recommendations for how to help this shift in teacher recruitment and retention occur. This was an acknowledgement that there were many teachers like Kimrey, who were leaving the teaching field.

Ten years after the No Child Left Behind Act, the Obama Administration introduced the American Reinvestment and Recovery Act (ARRA; United States Congress, 2009) in which professional development was outlined as an investment opportunity to jump-start school reform and improvement efforts. Many states applied for and were granted ARRA funds—all with individual and unique plans for teacher improvement. A year later, in the *Blueprint for School Reform* (U.S. Department of Education, 2010), a document that outlined the Obama administration's recommendations for the reauthorization of the Elementary and Secondary Education Act, professional development was once again highlighted as a critical component of school success. In 2015, the Every Student Succeeds Act (ESSA) reauthorized the Elementary and Secondary Education Act and defined professional development as strategies that provide educators "with the knowledge and skills necessary to enable students to succeed in a well-rounded education and to meet challenging State academic standards" (U.S. Congress, 2015).

Focus and funding for professional development has been at the helm of most reform efforts. However, in recent studies, professional development has not been shown to impact changes in teacher practice or student achievement. As an example, a large scale study found that teacher evaluations stayed the same or declined during the time span that districts spent more than $18,000 per teacher on professional development. While this is certainly troubling, the authors of this study did not recommend reducing the investment in teacher professional development, rather they recommended keep current levels of funding while at the same time encouraging leaders to consider redefining the structures and mechanisms of professional learning and how to support that learning at scale (The New Teacher Project, 2015).

In addition, it's clear that many other variations of reform, standards, teacher evaluation systems, new curriculum, assessment, or even funding, have barely moved the needle on actual classroom practice (Cuban, 2013). To this end, our goal is to explore effective strategies that result in teacher change. How do we redefine structures and mechanisms for professional learning at scale in order to make significant progress on changing classroom practice?

## PROFESSIONAL DEVELOPMENT VS. PROFESSIONAL LEARNING

As we consider how to make substantive change, we find it important to make the distinction between the terms, *professional development* and *professional learning*. Fullan (2007) describes the term *professional development* as "a major obstacle to progress in teacher learning" (p. 35). *Professional development* as a term, leads one to think of workshops, training days, and other instances where the focus is on delivering information *to* teachers, as opposed to considering whether or not teachers are learning anything that results in a shift in practice. Schools often find that professional development does not always lead to learning despite its intent (Easton, 2008; Fullan, 2007). While some professional development opportunities are well designed and take into consideration adult learning, they are not powerful enough to lead to sustained change.

> *The distinction between professional learning and professional development is more than semantics.*

Definitions of professional development have changed in recent years. Research on professional learning communities (PLCs) and other collaborative practices has been integrated into schools and districts. This change indicates a national movement toward the concept of continual learning and social contexts for teacher change—not "one and done" workshops. Therefore, Fraser, Kennedy, Reid, and Mckinney (2007) suggested that the term *professional learning* be used instead to describe these collaborative practices. They define them as processes "that, whether intuitive or deliberate, individual or social, result in specific changes in the professional knowledge, skills, attitudes, beliefs or actions of teachers" (p. 157). It is this definition that we subscribe to as we use the term *professional learning* throughout this book.

The evidence of the shift toward professional learning was solidified when the foremost authority on teacher professional learning, the National Staff Development Council, changed its name to Learning Forward in 2010 and renamed their *Standards for Professional Development* to *Standards for Professional Learning* in 2011. Executive Director of Learning Forward, Stephanie Hirsh (Learning Forward, 2011), described the shift in language as signaling "the importance of educators taking an active role in their continuous development and places an emphasis on their learning."

The shift from Learning Forward included more than a change in name. The new standards called forth collaboration and learning communities in a way that was different than in the past. Research around PLCs and other collaborative approaches to learning were more prevalent in the literature, and schools were considering the nature of job-embedded professional learning in ways that they hadn't in the past. Professional learning leaders were beginning to look at the standards and mechanisms for professional learning and reconsidering their approaches to teacher learning.

In addition to prominent organizations shifting, policy began to move as well. The Every Student Succeeds Act (ESSA) of 2015 prioritized professional learning that is woven into the school day and allows for collaboration. In fact, ESSA went as far as to redefine professional learning as sustained, intensive, collaborative, job-embedded, data-driven, and classroom-focused. This is a welcome evolution of research informing policy and practice. When combined with Learning Forward's *Standards for Professional Learning* (2011), both support professional learning as a critical strategy for improvement and require leaders to create systems that will achieve the intended outcomes (Hirsch, 2017).

Organizations and policies dramatically shifted their stance on what was important to consider in teacher recruitment, retention, and professional learning. This shift also intensified the need for professional learning that supports the changes we see in the complexity of student learning required for 21st-century competencies. Virtually all of the authoritative voices in every teaching field are calling for schools that are more experiential, authentic, collaborative, democratic, and challenging (Zemelman, Daniels, & Hyde, 2012).

> If "experiential, authentic, collaborative, democratic, and challenging" learning is expected for our students, our professional learning experiences should mirror that learning and support teachers to learn the pedagogy needed to teach these skills.

## DESIGNING LEARNING FOR ADULTS

As is often the case with students, teachers' learning needs vary widely. Our belief is that good instruction is good instruction—whether it is designed for youngsters or adult learners. Academic instruction drives both social and emotional development as well as learning. It constitutes most of what happens during the school day, and it greatly colors students' experiences of schooling. A steady diet of didactic instruction is frustrating, boring, and alienating and puts students in a passive sit-and-get role.

The same is true for the teachers with whom we work. Without frequent opportunities to be active, collaborative, and reflective in the learning process, many learners (both novice and more experienced) will not grow socially or academically. Therefore, in order to comfortably and successfully transform instructional practice, most teachers need extended professional learning opportunities that look like the learning experiences that are being promoted for students (Darling-Hammond, Hyler, & Gardner, 2017). Most districts underestimate this need, and they do not allocate the time, staffing, or resources necessary to provide it.

Understanding adult learners is one of the keys to school improvement through professional learning. Knowles's (1973) seminal work describes nine findings related to the optimal conditions for adult learners: control of their learning; immediate utility; focus on issues that concern them; test their learning as they go; anticipate how they will use their learning; expect performance improvement; maximize available resources; require collaborative, respectful, mutual, and informal climate; and rely on information that is appropriate and developmentally paced. Trotter (2006) built on Knowles's work, identifying three key themes that are important when designing professional learning for adults:

- Adults build from their own experiences.

- Adults need to plan their learning paths based on their interest and contexts.

- The aim of adult professional learning should be to promote inquiry and reflection.

Yet, understanding adult learning theory is only one part of the change process. In order for change to truly occur, one must attend to the hearts and minds of teachers (Hayes, 2008). Teachers "teach from what they understand and believe about learning, what they know how to do and what their environments will allow" (Darling-Hammond, 1996, p. 9). Often, teachers change their underlying beliefs only after they see success with students (Guskey, 2002), but student success is hard to see initially, and learning new teaching skills takes many attempts to master (Gulamhussein, 2013). Most teachers use a very narrow range of instructional practices (Sirotnik, 1983; Goodlad & Klein, 1970; Medley, 1977) and only expand that repertoire when they are provided carefully designed professional learning experiences. However carefully designed those learning experiences are, they are just the beginning of the change process.

## CONNECTING RESEARCH AND REALITY

Connecting professional learning to student achievement outcomes is one of the "holy grails" of education. In that vein, researchers and others have focused on understanding what characteristics or mechanisms of professional learning are necessary to make changes in teacher practice and student achievement. Recent research has identified various characteristics of effective professional learning, and the empirical base is gaining strength.

In a literature review, Yoon, Duncan, Lee, Scarloss, and Shapley (2007) found only nine studies of professional learning that had clear outcome measures of student achievement. More recently, Darling-Hammond et al. (2017) found thirty-five studies of professional learning that employed rigorous methodologies to show a positive link between teacher professional learning and student achievement. How do we ensure that all professional learning offers a positive impact on student achievement?

In 2009, Desimone suggested that there was a sufficient research base to support a set of features of professional learning that positively impacts teacher improvement and causally impacts student achievement. She identified content focus, active learning, coherence, duration, and collective participation as the research-based characteristics of professional learning. Desimone also proposed that there was sufficient empirical evidence to support these features and that further research should include this set of characteristics to begin to look for causal effects in student achievement.

Desimone's list encompasses some of the characteristics that are frequently discussed in a myriad of other menus of effective professional learning characteristics (American Federation of Teachers, 2002; Association for Supervision and Curriculum Design, 2002; Guskey, 2000; Wei, Darling-Hammond, Andree, Richardson, & Orphanos, 2009). Since Desimone's seminal article, the list of research-based characteristics has grown. A recent report suggests that there are seven characteristics of effective professional learning (Darling-Hammond et al., 2017):

1. Is content focused

2. Incorporates active learning utilizing adult learning theory

3. Supports collaboration, typically in job-embedded contexts,

4. Uses models and modeling of effective practice

5. Provides coaching and expert support

6. Offers opportunities for feedback and reflection

7. Is of sustained duration

Unfortunately, lists of professional learning characteristics leave instructional leaders, who are often tasked with designing and implementing professional learning, lacking for guidance.

Professional learning leaders must also consider how the essential characteristics are linked together while also making room for additional characteristics or features that may play an important role in teacher learning and student achievement.

> *Lists give the impression that if all of the necessary components are included, then professional learning is rigorous and leads to the desired outcomes. It is not enough to simply check off a list of essential characteristics of effective professional learning.*

In this vein, a recent review by Kennedy (2016) acknowledges that the bulk of research on professional learning has focused heavily on the essential characteristics of the learning itself rather than considering the variability in the content, design, and context. She noted, "We need to replace our current conception of 'good' PD as comprising a collection of particular design features with a conception that is based on more nuanced understanding of what teachers do, what motivates them, and how they learn and grow" (p. 974). Kennedy's stance is similar to our goals in this text. When designing learning experiences for adults, we must look closely at the research-based characteristics, but just as importantly, also consider the needs of the audience, the task, and the purpose.

*[handwritten margin note: what is good pd?]*

We have shared much of the research on effective professional learning for teachers that results in student success. It is critical for leaders of teacher learning to be familiar with what past studies have determined, but it is just as imperative for professional learning leaders to understand how to think about their own context for leading learning and determine strategies that will support their districts, their teachers, and ultimately, the students in classrooms. Through the research, vignettes, and tools we offer in this book, we hope our readers can find some nuggets to help them in their quest to lead learning—for both the educators and the students in our school systems.

For most educators, professional learning is the singular, most accessible means they have to develop the new knowledge, skills, and practices necessary to better meet students' learning needs. Focusing on professional learning as an approach to reform and school improvement is much more difficult than enacting a new program and teaching teachers how to implement it. Schools are complex ecosystems of students, families, teachers, staff, and community

*[handwritten margin note: purpose of PD is to better meet needs]*

members, making the task of designing a plan for professional learning, whether it is a multiyear system around a particular innovation or a single event, a difficult one. We must not only understand the important characteristics of effective professional learning, we also need to closely attend to the needs of our learners, the larger goals of the learning, and the smaller goals of the task at hand. In the subsequent chapters, we will make the case for taking into consideration the learning needs of individual participants, the overarching goals for shifting practice, and the goals of each specific experience.

## Questions for Reflection

- How do you, in your practice, reconcile the difference between professional development and professional learning?

- How does the current research on professional learning connect with reality in the setting in which you work?

- What might you want to consider when designing learning experiences for adults? How might you make the connection to student learning?

# CHAPTER 2

# Learning Within Content

It is clear that professional learning about general classroom practices does not lead to sustained teacher change or student achievement—moreover, professional learning opportunities that lack a content focus have little influence on student achievement. A rich and thoughtful content focus (for example, how young children learn foundational skills, comprehension strategies, the recursive nature of the writing process, etc.) during professional learning is tied to both change in teacher practice and student growth. To this end, curricular materials are often used to support both the content knowledge and pedagogy of teachers. Many times, however, curricular materials are often a forgotten part of the professional learning landscape. This chapter will explore the role of content focus and support of curricular materials in teachers' professional learning experiences.

> In order for improvement to take root, it is essential that professional learning focus on "learning to do the right things in the setting where you work."
>
> —Elmore, 2004, p. 73

## WHY IS CONTENT SO IMPORTANT?

The content of professional learning is most useful when it focuses on increasing teachers' subject area knowledge or pedagogical content knowledge and links that knowledge to classroom practice, rather than general learning or behavior techniques (Darling-Hammond & McLaughlin, 1995). Multiple studies show strong effects of professional learning on practice when it focuses on specific pedagogy, content, instructional techniques, and a focus on student learning of that specific content (Carpenter, Feneman, Peterson, Chiang, & Loef, 1989; Doppelt et al., 2009; Heller, Daehler, Wong, Shinohara, & Miratrix, 2012; Kennedy, 1998; Kim et al., 2011; Sloan, 1993). Professional learning that focuses on generic strategies or general principles that are divorced from their day-to-day practice is less likely to impact teachers' application of what they learn or improve student outcomes (Taylor et al., 2015).

A strong content focus is included on many lists as a characteristic of effective professional development (Darling-Hammond, Hyler, & Gardner, 2017; Guskey, 2000; Hill, 2004; Wei, Darling-Hammond, Andree, Richardson, & Orphanos, 2009). This characteristic is based on a belief that in order to teach effectively, teachers must have not only a solid understanding of the content they are conveying but also have a deep understanding of how children learn the content best and the common misconceptions students may have while learning the content (Antoniou & Kyriakides, 2013; Ball & Cohen, 1999; Bransford, Brown, & Cocking, 2000). Interestingly, content knowledge itself is not what makes the difference in student achievement. Many studies show that the professional learning must link content learning to the pedagogy that supports teachers' practice and student learning (Heller et al., 2012).

For example, literacy professional development, with a strong content focus on increasing teacher knowledge of language and children's reading and writing development, has been shown to have a positive impact on students' achievement (Landry, Anthony, Swank, & Monseque-Bailey, 2009; McCutchen et al., 2002; McGill-Franzen, Allington, Yokoi, & Brooks, 1999; Rosemary, Roskos, & Landreth, 2007; Van Keer & Verhaeghe, 2005). Specifically, McCutchen et al. (2002) found a significant increase in students' word reading after an intensive professional development experience that focused on both increasing teachers' knowledge of phonology and orthographics and linking that knowledge to pedagogy. This study along with others (Buysse, Castro, & Peisner-Feinberg, 2010; Johnson & Fargo, 2014) suggests that a strong content focus is effective only when the professional learning is directly linked to pedagogy and implications for classroom practice.

There is a large and growing body of educational research on effective classroom practices. Researchers, such as John Hattie (2009), have shown that we actually now know what to do to support student growth. Through professional learning opportunities, we need to offer educators the chance to learn from experts in the field. Sharing information that ever so slightly nudges our thinking (or even forcefully pushes our thinking) allows us to discover new ideas with support and then hopefully shift instructional practice. The resources that we explore to either nudge or push are called "conceptual inputs."

## USING CONCEPTUAL INPUTS

Conceptual inputs refer to outside resources designed to ground the learning in research or conceptual/theoretical basis. Professional learning cannot come without strong conceptual inputs as a way to link research and practice (Hoban, 2002).

Hill (2004) studied 13 different professional development sessions to see if they met the standards for high-quality professional development. Her findings indicated the content presented was "mediocre," and there was no "rich and robust treatment of instruction" (p. 222). Additionally, when surveying teachers about their professional development, findings indicated that "intellectual content (was) often thin" (Little et al., 1987, p. 17). Professional learning that has strong conceptual inputs as part of its design allows for innovations to be tried on a solid base of theory and links that theory to actual classroom practice.

Conceptual inputs can take many forms. The simplest is a professional reading based in research—a recent book, an article, or an educational brief. Using a professional journal article or a book to spark new understandings supports teachers in understanding the theory behind a new way of work. Another example of a conceptual input could be what Vygotsky (1978) calls a "more knowledgeable other"—someone who has a better understanding with a particular task or concept. Sometimes these "more knowledgeable others" are colleagues and coaches situated in our schools or districts. It's clear that outside experts play an important role. Guskey and Yoon (2009) found that when professional learning experiences were facilitated by an outside expert who also supported the work within the school context there were greater improvements in student learning.

Partnerships with professors at a local university can serve as conceptual inputs in a district's professional learning plan. Many demonstrated instances of strong conceptual inputs that impacted student achievement have resulted from professional learning situated within a university-school partnership (Carpenter et al., 1989; Desimone, Porter, Garet, Yoon, & Birman, 2002; Duffy et al., 1986; Harwell, D'Amico, Stein, & Gatti, 2000; Landry et al., 2009; McCutchen et al., 2002; McGill-Franzen et al., 1999; Neale, Smith, & Johnson, 1990; Rosemary et al., 2007; Van Keer & Verhaeghe, 2005). In addition to outside experts, "inside" experts in the form of coaches or other teachers can be models as well.

*When coaches have deep understandings of content and pedagogy, they can support teachers in unpacking how particular aspects of instruction can be used to meet student needs.*

To explore this, take a moment and consider the following case study.

Lindsey, a school-based instructional coach, has been working with the K–2 teachers to implement a foundational skills program that uses clear and concise routines for phonological awareness, letter sounds, decoding, sight words, and fluency. The program was designed to support teachers in allowing the students to do most of the work without significant scaffolding. During classroom observations, Lindsey noticed that many teachers were still doing much of the "heavy lifting" for the students by sounding out words with them or providing lots of previewing.

The K–2 teachers reported that their lessons were taking much longer than the time allotted, and Lindsey knew that this time issue was due to lack of understanding of how to implement the routines. Lindsey also understood that if the teachers had a lack of understanding in implementing the routines, it could also indicate a lack of content knowledge and how students learn that content best.

She suggested a few rounds of side-by-side coaching. This structure allowed her to work directly with a teacher individually to support his or her understanding and implementation right in the moment. She had employed this method many times, and teachers found it very supportive since it was right in the context that they themselves would be implementing the strategies.

For the first round, Lindsey met with Beth, a first-grade teacher, to co-plan the small group lesson. They discussed where they thought the students might struggle and what routines would support them. Lindsey and Beth were able to consider the supports within the curriculum as well as discuss the instructional moves Beth might make given her knowledge of her students. This allowed them both to think about the instructional moves as well as the pacing to keep the lesson short and intense. Beth noted that a particular area of need was the sight word routine and the decoding new words routine, and they agreed to focus on those parts of the lesson.

The expectation was that the students were to review known sight words and employ a "read-spell-read" routine. Many teachers were adding in additional instruction, and the amount of teacher talk versus student talk was significant. Since the goal of sight word knowledge is automaticity, adding in additional language minimized the instructional power of the routine. Additionally, that added significant time to the lesson since teachers were often elaborating on every word that was to be practiced. For decoding new words, the routine was similar here, too. Teachers were adding additional language and many times articulating the sounds alongside the students making it difficult to discern if the students themselves were able to do the work.

Lindsey and Beth discussed each routine in depth. Lindsey helped Beth understand the reasoning behind the routine. Students were getting practice in the reciprocal processes of decoding and encoding when they engaged in read-spell-read. If teachers added additional language, the rhythm and repetition that supported the automaticity of that word was interrupted. Beth shared that she hadn't really thought about it like that before. She thought that by adding in other ways of thinking about the word, she was taking advantage of a "teachable moment." Lindsey and Beth then discussed the decoding words routine and had a similar conversation. The pedagogical moves in the routines were to support student ownership and to move the teacher to the role of coach. Through the discussion, Beth was able to unpack the content learning she needed to understand the instructional moves.

Lindsey and Beth cotaught the lesson the next day. Beth started the lesson by sharing with the students that she and Lindsey were trying some new things today and would talk to each other about their learning during the lesson. This not only gave the students an opportunity to see their teachers continually learning, it set up the idea that the lesson was going to be a bit different.

Beth started out with the sight-word routine and immediately implemented the routine as she and Lindsey had discussed the prior day during planning. She told the students that she was going to say three words only as they practiced their sight words, "read, spell, read." The students were ready, and Beth made it through the list efficiently. As soon as the routine ended, she turned to Lindsey, and they had a brief discussion of how the routine went differently this time.

Next it was Lindsey's turn to implement the decoding new words routine while Beth took the role of observer. Lindsey also implemented the routine as discussed, but the students struggled significantly without the additional scaffolding. Lindsey and Beth conferred in the moment and decided to change the pacing for the first few words, so the students could get used to a less scaffolded routine. It was clear to Beth that her previous way of teaching this routine had oversupported her students, and they were not as independent as she wanted them to be. This opportunity to work side-by-side with Lindsey had illuminated an aspect of her teaching that she had not previously recognized.

This vignette showcases two parts of content-based professional learning. First, Beth had Lindsey as a knowledgeable other who had knowledge of how and why the routines were designed the way they were and how they might maximize student ownership of the learning. Second, the curriculum itself was a conceptual input that both Lindsey and Beth used to support their learning. Deepening the understanding of the "why" behind the instructional moves supported Beth in her implementation, and by engaging in this model with Lindsey, together they were able to see how those moves support student learning.

## How Might We Partner With Our Curriculum?

As showcased above, a component of content-based professional learning and a conceptual input could include the curricular materials that teachers teach with every day. As we consider situating experiences in teachers' own contexts, curricular materials are an important consideration. Many of us have been in professional learning sessions where we were learning new teaching techniques or strategies only to know that we would have difficulty enacting them in our classrooms where mandated curricular materials do not support those new practices.

When we consider professional learning at scale, we must consider the role of curricular materials. Inherently, materials are already a part of the routine of school and have a central role in the instructional system (Ball & Cohen, 1996). Yet, current practice often separates "what we teach" (curriculum) from "how we teach" (professional learning), which undermines the effectiveness of both (Wiener & Pimentel, 2017). As we consider content-specific professional learning, we must consider the tools that teachers have at their disposal every day.

A key component of professional learning is to support teachers in envisioning new instructional models, strategies, and techniques. As we revisit adult learning theory, we know that teachers need to see immediate utility in what they are learning and build from their own experiences. Linking professional learning to the materials that teachers use every day can support them in envisioning a different kind of instruction and scaffolding their attempts with their students (Gallagher, 2016).

Often, curriculum materials are part of a process to improve instruction, but the "adoption of new materials is rarely seen as one component of a systemic approach to professional development" (Ball & Cohen, 1996, p. 7). When the materials adopted are of high quality and seek to serve in an educative role, they can serve as a tool for changed practice when combined with professional learning. High-quality instructional materials serve as that rich thoughtful content that research has proven to be critical to supporting teacher change.

While there is conflicting information about whether or not curriculum is a change agent in itself, we know that when paired with professional learning, curriculum can serve as a powerful tool for teacher change. Several studies have shown that teachers who receive high-quality curricular materials have lower student achievement than those who have both the curricular materials and professional learning that supports their attempts at new ways to facilitate student learning (Doppelt et al., 2009; Kleickmann, Trobst, Jonen, Vehmeyer, & Moller, 2016). Even more significant is the suggestion that students have better outcomes if their teachers do not attempt a new curriculum without the accompanying professional learning to support them (Darling-Hammond et al., 2017).

While processes to support the marriage of curricular materials and professional learning will be explored deeply in Chapter 4, we know that the conversation about how to use high-quality curricular materials as conceptual inputs for professional learning is important. Stephanie Hirsch, director of Learning Forward, recently published a column (Hirsch, 2018) that outlines the understanding of curricular materials as partners in professional learning. "The place where that comes together in schools is through grade-level, subject-specific professional learning communities that enable teachers to plan, execute, and assess how a district or school curriculum is working for students over the course of a year." Using high-quality curricular materials as conceptual inputs supports teacher learning in many ways, the first of which is increasing their content knowledge. High-quality curricula include a level of transparency around the content knowledge teachers need to successfully teach a particular subject. For example, in a unit on making inferences, the curriculum developer added this in the teacher materials:

> Not everything communicated by a text is directly stated. Good readers use their prior knowledge and the information in a text to understand implied meanings. Making inference helps readers move beyond the literal to a deeper understanding of texts. In Making Meaning grade 4, the students make inferences to think more deeply about both narrative and expository texts (Center for the Collaborative Classroom, 2015).

The curriculum developers want to help teachers understand why readers infer and how it deepens comprehension. This support, at the point of need for teachers, helps them increase their content knowledge within the materials they use every day.

You may have noticed that we use the term "high quality" when describing the curricular materials used as a conceptual input in professional learning. This is not by accident.

The example above showcases one part of an educative curriculum. It supports teachers' content knowledge of the material they are teaching. Educative curriculum support teacher learning in others ways, too. Consider the following case study.

*While some curricular materials are designed to be "teacher-proof," others are designed to support teachers' thinking and learning while implementing an innovation or change. The design of "educative curricula" is in many ways the actualization of professional learning.*

A medium-sized suburban school district had been analyzing teacher observation data and noticed that many teachers needed support in asking open-ended questions. Understanding that professional learning must be content focused, the district tasked content-area specialists to design professional learning that supported this instructional strategy but situated it specifically in the content arena that teachers would be expected to use it. Jason, an English Language Arts (ELA) specialist, considered a series of modified lesson study experiences that would focus directly on using open-ended questions during interactive read alouds and discussing text. The district had recently purchased an educative reading comprehension curriculum to support teachers in deepening their knowledge of comprehension strategy instruction, and Jason knew that open-ended questions were a big part of that instructional design.

He began working with grade-level teams at a single school. The modified lesson study he designed used the curricular materials as a basis for learning. As a frame for the experience, he expected to engage teachers in a discussion of how the intended instructional strategy had been going, then move into planning a lesson collaboratively using the instructional materials focusing on the open-ended questions, then he would teach the lesson as planned by the team, and finally debrief the experience together. After this initial experience, the team would meet twice more during the school year, and teachers would take on the teaching of the modeled lessons themselves. Jason planned this series of experiences so that they could dig deeply into open-ended questioning techniques while recognizing the power of the educative curriculum as a resource for supporting their own learning.

He began by asking the teachers to consider how class discussions had been going for the past few weeks. Teachers remarked that the students were engaged in the discussions, but it felt more like a "back and forth" between the teacher and the students rather than a deep discussion between the students themselves. Jason asked the teachers to reflect on the reasons why that might be the case.

**Olga:** I think the kids don't have the language necessary to really engage in a real discussion. They just use one- or two-word answers to my question.

**Sal:** I agree with Olga. I think we're expecting too much of fourth graders.

**Kizzie:** I've actually noticed something a little different. Sometimes, it seems like the discussions go really well, and the kids have a lot to say, but other times I feel like I have to really fill in a lot of gaps in the conversation or do a lot of telling.

**Jason:** Kizzie, have you noticed what makes it go better sometimes rather than others?

**Kizzie:** Not exactly, but I think I've realized that sometimes I ask a question that doesn't really lead to the kind of discussion that I want the kids to have. I'm wondering if the way I ask the question is what's determining their level of engagement or access to the discussion?

**Jason:** Let's build off of what Kizzie just said. When you're asking questions during the interactive read aloud portion of the lesson, how are the kids responding?

**Olga:** Those seem to go a bit better than the discussions. I think the kids are really engaged with the read aloud, so they seem to be better able to answer them.

**Kizzie:** I agree with Olga, but I also think that sometimes the kids think they're just supposed to answer the question and not really discuss it.

**Sal:** Yes, I think the kids wait for me to say that they're right, and there's really no exploration. I know the curriculum asks us to probe, but sometimes I don't even know what to probe for!

Based on the initial reflections, Jason led the teachers into the materials for the lesson that was to be taught that day. The teachers and Jason together broke each section of the lesson down and discussed what students were expected to know and do in that part of the lesson and how each section led to the next. Jason and the teachers planned for how they would respond to students if misconceptions arose and how they would frame each part of the lesson. The team paid particular attention to the questions that were posed during an interactive reading of the text and the discussion.

**Jason:** What do you notice about the way the questions are posed in this part of the lesson?

**Sal:** They're very open ended, so there's no "right" answer.

**Olga:** I think sometimes the way the questions are written in the manual are too confusing for the kids, so I change it a bit?

**Jason:** Can you say more about that?

**Olga:** Sure, look at this one. The question says, "Is the setting an important part of this story? Why do you think so?" I think that's a lot of words, so I would just say, "What is the setting?" and after a few kids answered, I would say "Is the setting important to the story?"

**Kizzie:** Well, if you change the questions like that, it really changes how kids will answer it.

**Olga:** How? The most important thing to know is setting and if it's important.

**Kizzie:** I think that the way the question is worded in the manual allows for kids to explore the "why" behind their thinking. If we just ask them about the setting and then if it's important, we never really get to their thinking. I'm realizing now how the open-ended nature of the questions allows for more than one opinion and really helps kids develop the conversation deeper.

Jason allowed the discussion to evolve for a bit, and the teachers began to understand how their own intentional or unintentional rephrasing of the questions from open to closed was hindering the students' discussion. They agreed in their planning that Jason, as the model teacher today, would ask the questions exactly as written. The teachers, as the observers for today's lesson, would collect data on the students' responses.

Jason taught the lesson as collaboratively planned, and the teachers collected data on student responses after the open-ended questions were posed. They came back together to analyze their data and debrief the experience.

**Kizzie:** I had a total aha moment while I was watching the lesson. Remember when I said that sometimes the discussions go better when I pose the questions during the read aloud rather than after the reading? Well, I think that's because I'm more careful with my language during the read aloud, and I kind of "wing it" for the discussion after the reading.

**Jason:** Say more about that, Kizzie.

**Kizzie:** Well, I often write the questions right out of the manual and put them on a sticky note in my book during an interactive read aloud. I think I'm actually copying the question as written. When I do the discussions after the reading, though, I think I just get the gist of the question and then go for it. I'm realizing that I'm not as precise with my words, so the kids don't really know what or how to discuss it.

**Olga:** I was really blown away by the quality of the kids' responses. Listening to Kizzie, I'm thinking that because I kind of "dumb down" the language, I'm actually changing the trajectory of the conversations. I was really surprised that they were able to say so much during the discussion. I really thought that if Jason asked the questions as they were written, they were going to be too hard. I think I really need to change some of my expectations.

**Sal:** Once again, I agree with Olga. I don't think I realized that many times I'm changing the questions from open ended to closed. I think out of force of habit, I'm actually asking a ton of questions that could really just be answered with a "yes" or "no," and we know that doesn't lead to deep thinking!

Jason wrapped up these reflections with a call to action. He asked the team to consider asking the questions exactly as written for the next full unit. In their next experience, they would debrief the student responses during that unit and consider next steps. Jason was hopeful that this experience was the beginning of shifting the teacher language around questioning.

As we unpack the case study, we can see illustrated the power of the conceptual input, an educative curriculum, in moving professional learning deeper. Because Jason had a resource at the ready that incorporated the teaching technique he wanted to promote, he was able to not only use that during a professional learning experience, but the materials themselves served as ongoing professional learning that the teachers were learning from as they engaged in the next unit. As Michael Fullan says, "Implementation is professional learning" (Fullan, Hord, & von Frank, 2015, p. 3). In addition, Jason was able to situate the teachers' learning in the content area in which they were responsible for using it. Consider an alternative situation where an external person came and delivered a session on the importance of open-ended questions and then had teachers practice writing them in various subject areas. Unfortunately, that is the scenario in many places. Jason knew that if he really wanted teachers' instruction to change, he needed to provide them with an experience that built off their own existing knowledge, using materials they already had, and with their own students.

Consider the chart on the next page as a guide for planning professional learning alongside curricular resources. Notice how salient features present in the curriculum can serve as the basis of experiences for teachers to build from. You also might see how the design of the professional learning experiences are particularly supportive for the element addressed and that a single experience is never the breadth of the work. A tool like this can be helpful in considering whether or not you can use your curricular tool for ongoing support. You will find a blank planning tool in Appendix 1.

## CURRICULAR RESOURCE PLANNING TOOL

This planning tool can help guide your thinking around how to use the curricular materials at hand to support teacher learning. It also helps you consider if the materials you have are meeting your goals for teaching and learning. When the gap between the materials given to support teachers and students and the instruction we want them experience is wide, teachers have to invent their own pathways, and most of the time, they do that alone (Ball & Cohen, 1996). When quality materials are used to support teacher learning in collaborative contexts, we are ensuring that they find coherence among their tools. Additionally, planning for such learning maximizes resources (both human and material) and allows for a more cohesive learning experience.

## WHAT ARE THE IMPLICATIONS FOR INSTRUCTIONAL PRACTICE?

Think about your own professional learning experiences. We often ask teachers to describe the most powerful professional learning experience they have participated in and what made it so powerful. Take a minute to reflect before you read any further. What professional learning experience has been the most powerful for you?

Many colleagues we work with comment on their Reading Recovery training. Reading Recovery is a highly effective short-term intervention of one-to-one tutoring for low-achieving first graders and requires intensive professional learning on the part of the teacher. When becoming Reading Recovery teachers, not only are participants immersed in critically

| INSTRUCTIONAL STRATEGY | DOES THE CURRICULUM ADDRESS THIS STRATEGY? IF NOT, HOW WILL IT BE ADDED? | HOW THE CURRICULUM ADDRESSES THE STRATEGY | POSSIBLE MISCONCEPTIONS/ AREAS OF GROWTH | PROFESSIONAL LEARNING EXPERIENCES | ONGOING LEARNING |
|---|---|---|---|---|---|
| Chunking content | Y | Each lesson builds upon the next. Consider the arc of instruction and a week of instruction and a unit. | Teachers might pick and choose lessons because they don't understand how the content develops across time. | Collaborative planning sessions. Support teachers' understanding of the unit/week/day design. | Teachers will engage in collaborative planning sessions every five weeks over the course of the school year. |
| Student-student interaction | Y | Time for collaborative conversations are built into every lesson every day. | Teachers sometimes feel as though they don't have time for this. They could skip the collaborative parts. | Lesson study experiences— Teachers can attempt building in the collaborative time and analyzing the time spent. | Three lesson study cycles per year focused on varying aspects of student-student interactions. |
| Probing misconceptions | N—Teachers need support in language that will probe misconceptions while allowing the students to retain ownership of the learning. | | Teacher language used to probe misconceptions is not allowing students to do the thinking. | Shared video analysis. Teachers consider the language used and how to add that to their discussions. | This aspect of learning will be added to the collaborative planning sessions above. |

important content about how children learn to read but also learning techniques and strategies for teaching their most struggling students. Participants are required to teach approximately four students in the one-on-one setting during this training year. They attend "behind the glass" sessions, and one teacher brings a student to each session and teaches a lesson behind a one-way mirror so that the rest of the class can learn from the instruction. The year-long training to become a Reading Recovery teacher is a strong illustration of learning techniques and strategies within the content area that they will be applied.

Often times, a general instructional strategy, like asking open-ended questions in the previous case study, is identified as a need in a school or district. We can consider many of Hattie's (2009) high-impact strategies as those that often are important across content areas. One way to position that "general learning" is as an initiating event, and most subsequent learning happens in a content-specific domain. For example, as districts and schools across the United States grapple with equity in education, there is a tendency to bring in authors or speakers to share their knowledge with the whole school/district. While this might be a motivating and enlightening event, as a stand-alone session, it is unlikely to lead to significant change in practice.

However, if that event is positioned within the context of many other job-embedded learning opportunities, participating teachers might successfully make much needed instructional shifts. For instance, a district might choose to bring an esteemed author/researcher in to speak to the entire staff in August during the beginning of the school year. Then, content facilitators at the district level offer, throughout the school year, opportunities for subsequent learning in their content-specific areas. For example, the ELA coordinator might schedule after-school sessions once a month with her K–6 teachers looking at a variety of children's books to ensure diverse representation. The social studies coordinator may offer several lesson study cycles that look closely at lessons focused on marginalized groups during world events. The math and science coordinator might create an online course exploring collaborative groupings during math that ensure that all students have a voice. If the work is continued throughout the school year in this vein, then the likelihood that that instructional practice will be incorporated into teachers' daily work is much higher. The bottom line is that teachers need support in understanding both why and how instructional shifts are necessary, and they learn that best within the content they teach.

The research makes it clear that not only is content essential, but how to best deliver that content to students is important—the two go hand-in-hand. As leaders of teacher learning, we need to offer the why and share the how at the same time—particularly citing strategies and practices that mirror the content.

We embed in our lessons multiple opportunities for students to turn and talk to one another about their thinking. But, we need to understand why that is important so that we offer time to turn and talk intentionally. Giving learners the chance for oral rehearsal, building the community in our classrooms, and helping students take risks are inherently smart experiences for students—the chance to turn and talk with a partner about a big idea allows for these experiences.

*A deep understanding of the why along with the how will allow us to use instructional strategies in our classrooms with thoughtful intent and success.*

Understanding the "why" can be as simple as taking the time to read and reflect on the current research behind our instructional practices and engaging in dialogue to better our understanding. Then, once we have a better sense of the "why," we can explore the new instructional techniques in classrooms through modeling, observation, and practice.

Following a simple structure to keep aspects of professional learning (content and strategy) in mind when planning is helpful. We have created a simple tool that you might find useful to guide your planning for short professional learning sessions (see Appendix 2). If we have a short amount of time with a group of educators, we might begin the professional learning experience by setting the stage. As a group, we can brainstorm, chart, or visualize what we want to know about the topic we are discussing. Then, through some sort of conceptual input, we can explore the "why." We need to explore what the research tells us about the topic through conceptual inputs in order to support our learning and push our thinking.

And most importantly, we need to see the learning in action in classrooms. We can do this through videotaped lessons or observations. We can also experience the learning ourselves through lesson experiences. We can read lesson plans and explore student work (see Chapter 3 for more active learning experiences). Then, we need to make time to reflect on our observations and make the learning our own through conversations with others and time to practice. Take a moment, and reflect on the following vignette about a professional learning day that Sarah facilitated focused on best practices in writing. She intentionally designed the day so that teachers have the chance to learn from more experienced others through readings and conversations. She also built in time for her participants to experience and reflect on several thoughtfully designed writing lessons—some that she taught herself to the participants and some that were videotaped lessons the group watched together.

Sarah had been working with a district for several years that hoped that their teachers would begin to use a workshop structure in their math classrooms. Writing workshop is one of the district's curricular requirements for teachers. The district does not mandate many instructional practices, but they do require writing workshop with the hope that the same structure will carry over into other parts of the instructional day. To this end, every fall and spring, they asked Sarah to facilitate a one-day workshop on best practices in mathematics instruction with a focus on the workshop structure.

The district leaders hoped that by experiencing this one-day workshop, teachers will understand the why behind their instruction—in both content areas. Teams of teachers self-select into these workshops in both the fall and spring—many new teachers attend, but oftentimes there are some teachers who have been teaching for awhile who either want a refresher or have only recently decided to embrace a workshop approach. Sarah designed the workshop so that there are multiple conceptual inputs around the best practices in mathematics instruction.

During the day, teachers read seminal research articles that described what studies have told us should and should not be happening in their elementary math classrooms. They discussed quotes written by professional authors in the field in order to better understand their thinking on workshops within the context of the math instruction. There were multiple opportunities for participants to experience a lesson and problem solve independently around content that is appropriate for their age group or to participate in an engaging protocol or technique that they could take back and explore in their classrooms. They watched video of several lessons in action and discussed what they noticed about the student learning as well as the teacher-led instruction. Sarah also shared a structure for conferring that teachers can use in their own math conferences.

There are several important elements missing from this professional learning model; however, the district has done one very important thing. They offer teachers the content they need to understand (the "gentle push") and successfully implement a math workshop approach in their classroom. They situate this workshop within the content (math and writing) the teachers are expected to use it.

As you've read in this chapter, situating professional learning within the content that teachers will use it and combining that with conceptual inputs that push the thinking further is a critical part of professional learning. But, it is just that—one part. For professional learning to truly take root, other elements are necessary to bring the learning to life. As implied through the tools, vignettes, and examples in this chapter, active learning, coherence, collaboration, and duration are other essential ingredients in bringing teacher learning to fruition. It is through those design elements that the content of professional learning comes to life.

- In what ways does content knowledge support the necessary learning for classroom change?

- How are you currently addressing content in the professional learning you are offering teachers?

- How does professional learning support the implementation of curriculum in the setting in which you work?

- How does your current adopted curriculum support your professional learning? How might you make the connection more overt?

# CHAPTER 3

# Elements of Learning

Let's now consider what the research suggests about the professional learning experiences that educators engage in and how they make an impact on changes in practice and, ultimately, student achievement. In this chapter, the research-based features of thoughtful professional learning are defined. We will explore each feature individually and consider how that feature can be used in designing learning experiences for teachers. While the mechanisms for bringing these features to life (i.e., professional learning communities, coaching) are described in detail in Chapter 4, illustrations of how the features interact are used to support understanding. We will describe the kinds of activities that support and use these characteristics and offer questions to use as a guide when planning. Finally, we will think about some of the different processes that might support the professional learning you lead in the setting where you work.

> You cannot have students as continuous learners and effective collaborators, without teachers having these same characteristics.
>
> —Sarason, 1990

## FEATURES OF PROFESSIONAL LEARNING—WHAT DOES THE LEARNING LOOK LIKE AND SOUND LIKE?

As described in Chapter 2, situating professional learning experiences for educators within their content domain is essential, but the ways in which we engage participants in the learning is equally as important. Emerging research has begun to deepen our collective understanding of what characteristics lead to transfer into teachers' practice and eventually into student achievement (Darling-Hammond, Hyler, & Gardner, 2017). The following features of powerful learning have a strong research base to support their use.

> While each feature of powerful learning is important, it is the collective power of the interaction of these features that truly supports teacher learning.

## ACTIVE LEARNING

Active learning is an essential characteristic of effective professional learning (Darling-Hammond et al., 2017; Desimone, 2009). Active learning refers to participants being engaged in their learning through observations, discussions, planning, and practice. This characteristic is in direct contrast to the "sit and get," passive learning models that have been typically promoted in professional development. Active learning can be considered an "umbrella element that often incorporates the elements of collaboration, coaching, feedback, and reflection and the use of models and modeling" (Darling-Hammond et al., 2017, p. 7). Meaningful active learning occurs when the instructional emphasis is on deep, rich understanding, and the learners are both actively engaged in constructing knowledge and provided many opportunities to apply newly learned skills (Bransford, Brown, & Cocking, 2000).

Effective professional learning offers us the opportunity to both construct our own knowledge and apply a new skill—all in turn leading to the ultimate goal of deep understanding. Toward this end, professional learning must mimic effective instructional classroom structures like investigation, inquiry, analysis, and critical habits of mind (Ball & Cohen, 1999). For example, many secondary English teachers follow Tom Romano's (2000) advice to assign a multigenre research project to their students. Rather than assign a traditional research paper—a single piece of writing about a particular a topic—they ask students to create a multigenre research project (a collection of pieces cohesively written in a variety of genres about a topic of their choosing and interest). This multigenre project can be used during a professional learning experience as well—offering teachers the opportunity to both construct knowledge about a topic they are interested in while at the same time practicing the skill of writing. Consider Robert's experience using the multigenre project with his graduate-level teachers.

Robert offers the same experience to his graduate-level teachers during a semester-long writing course. He offers practicing teachers the chance to experience and craft a multigenre research project around a topic of their own choosing (conferring, poetry, grammar instruction, etc.) just as English teachers might provide students the same opportunity in their classrooms. When teachers leave the class, they share feedback on their personal growth as writers. Consider the following quotes:

- "I believe I have developed as a teacher of writing through the things I have learned this semester but also as a writer."

- "From this course, I have learned a lot about myself as a writer and as a teacher of writing. I think the most valuable thing we can do to improve our teaching is to experience something ourselves in order to understand the challenges and process involved. We ask our students to go outside of their comfort zone and push them to think about and explore new ideas. Doing this myself for this class was very eye opening. Although I have learned a lot about how to teach writing, this was the first time I got to reflect on what it means to be a writer myself and how to relate to my students' experience. I really enjoyed writing the personal narratives pieces and weaving in aspects of my own life with my educational goals and experiences."

- "In reflecting on my learning over the course of the semester, I have grown as a writer and as a teacher of writing. Through [this class], I found myself enjoying writing again as I was composing pieces that interested me, encouraged me to reflect on myself as a person and teacher, and benefitted my teaching practices. I want to spread the joy I have found in writing and the rewards that come with it to my students."

During this professional learning experience, Robert immersed teachers in the process of understanding themselves as writers while at the same time allowing them to experience an instructional strategy that they could employ with their students. Many studies support the use of the same learning strategies and experiences that students would experience in professional learning for teachers (Buczynski & Hansen, 2010; Greenleaf et al., 2011; Heller, Daehler, Wong, Shinohara, & Miratrix, 2012). In order to successfully transform their practice, teachers need extended professional learning that looks like the learning experiences that are being promoted. The quotes from the teachers show the power of engaging in work that is similar to that of their students.

Teacher as Writer is an integral part of the National Writing Project's professional learning model (Whitney, 2008). During summer institutes and ongoing learning, there is dedicated time for teachers to engage in the writing process themselves and with peers. Process-oriented pedagogy supports that "we have to see ourselves as writers if we are to teach writing well" (Routman, 2004, p. 35). While the vignette and supporting quotes are specific to writing instruction and teachers engaging in that area themselves, the same holds true across reading as well. To that end, consider Arrica's engagement when reading a professional book and how this experience both changed her as a reader and supported her professional learning.

While reading *Mosaic of Thought* (Keene & Zimmerman, 2007) for the first time many years ago, Arrica was struck by the way Keene and Zimmerman embedded passages from adult literature to show how adult readers use comprehension strategies to support their own understanding of text. For her, this was the first time that she really had an opportunity to be metacognitive about how she was reading and interacting with the text. This was very powerful for Arrica, not only as a teacher of reading but as a reader herself. After reading *Mosaic of Thought*, Arrica became a deeper and more engaged reader, and that impacted her thinking, learning, and instruction significantly.

As we consider the reading experience above, we can't help but consider how to provide similar opportunities for teachers in the field. While Arrica's experience was a personally driven learning experience, we can engage groups of participants in similar structures.

*When we embed professional readings into our learning experiences and offer time with discussion protocols and other structures to engage in the text and the meaning, we are making transparent the kind of experiences that we want our students to have with text.*

Teachers engaging in reading and writing as part of their own professional learning serves multiple purposes. Readings can take the form of conceptual inputs to push our thinking. Discussing with others and writing in response to reading allows us to deepen our knowledge while also engaging as a learner in structures that could be supportive for students as well. When professional learning mirrors the student experiences we hope to create, teachers inherently have a deeper understanding of the feelings and effects on the learning that the experience creates. Understanding how students might feel has the potential to elevate teachers' commitment to change since they are able to understand firsthand how active learning supports deep learning.

Active learning is not just the way that content is presented and the corresponding activities, but it also includes connections to teachers' own contexts. Harken back to the Elmore quote that began Chapter 2: "*In order for improvement to take root, it is essential that professional learning focus on 'learning to do the right things in the setting where you work'*" (Elmore, 2004, p. 73). Teachers need to have their learning experiences in the very context that they are expected to enact change. In professional learning settings, these active learning structures might take form as rich discussions that situate new learning in the classroom context through observations of other teachers' practice. Active learning includes experiences where teachers come together to discuss problems of practice, analyze student work samples, and engage in learning that is directly related to their students and their experiences.

Because of the content addressed, active learning might look slightly different in the context of a primary classroom than it does in a session designed for adult learners. However, no matter the age level of the learner or the different experiences, both groups need to make sense of the world around them through engaging with others as well as engaging with rigorous content. We should hear that "busy hum" both during a first grade center time when students are sharing their thinking about their science learning as well as in the professional development resource center, media center, or a colleague's classroom when educators have gathered to think more deeply about pressing issues they face instructionally.

Active learning seems simple to plan and organize for young children and perhaps a bit more complicated to facilitate for adults. Being thoughtful about the different possibilities and activities to enhance the learning situation is critical for facilitators of adult learning.

> *When we are thoughtful in our planning of active learning for teachers, we support teachers in actually transforming their teaching and not simply adding another strategy (as we often hear) to "their repertoire" or "toolbag."*

## COHERENCE

In order for professional learning to make an impact, it must be embedded into the "day-to-day cultures of schools, districts, and the larger system" (Fullan, Hord, & von Frank, 2015, p. 5). It must have coherence. Coherence with district and school goals and state and national reform efforts has an impact on teacher learning and causally on student achievement. District decision making on professional learning offerings has considerable influence on the kinds of opportunities teachers may choose to attend, as well as shaping the goals for teacher learning. Firestone, Mangin, Martinez, & Polovsky (2005) studied the impact of a statewide professional learning effort on three different districts in New Jersey. Their findings indicated that district leadership has a profound impact on the professional learning offerings within the district, and each district's interpretation of the state policy was directly tied to the effectiveness of the professional learning. Although Firestone et al. did not examine differences in student achievement, only one district aligned its professional learning and school support with statewide efforts. As a consequence, only the teachers in that district reported greater understanding of the subject matter and how it related to their teaching.

While coherence at the national, state, and district levels impacts teacher learning and student achievement, coherence with the goals of school administration is also powerful. Several professional learning studies designed to measure perceived principal or school-level support showed an increase in teacher learning and student achievement (Banilower, Heck, & Weiss, 2007; Desimone, Porter, Garet, Yoon, & Birman, 2002; Garet, Porter, Desimone, Birman, & Yoon, 2001; Harwell, D'Amico, Stein, & Gatti, 2000). Clearly, coherence with teachers' prior knowledge, state and district reform efforts, and administrative goals determines the effectiveness of professional learning and its impact on teacher knowledge and student achievement.

Opportunities for district office staff to engage with teachers in buildings and for principals to connect with district leaders are critical to the healthy growth of a school district. Smart leadership teams know to keep their learning goals connected—from the office of the superintendent to the office of the building principals to the classroom teacher—always providing the chance for us to learn and grow together around similar learning targets. This allows for both individual and system learning to occur deeply around a connected topic.

Coherence also reminds us to think about how all the initiatives that are happening in schools, districts, and states need to be mutually supportive. Many districts and schools often have multiple change initiatives happening at the same time. Teachers can have a hard time deciphering how a new innovation fits into the current mandates. In fact, one school compared the professional learning and initiatives in their district to Baskin Robbins and their famous thirty-one flavors. The faculty felt as though whatever new thing any leader heard about became the next innovation that required new professional learning. The leadership was having difficulty explaining the interconnectedness of the initiatives, and the teachers were frustrated. It was a vivid reminder that if teachers are seeing such disconnection between their day-to-day work and the work at the whole school or district level, the learning is diminished. It is important for us to make connections between the professional learning we are supporting and the ongoing processes teachers have been engaged in.

One way to illustrate this is to consider a district that has been actively promoting the use of balanced literacy instruction for a number of years and now a new teacher evaluation model is introduced. If the professional learning around the new teacher evaluation model does not overtly connect how balanced literacy is supported within the new evaluation, teachers may feel as though they are being asked to teach in new ways. If we are able to show alignment between these initiatives, teachers have a much better chance of actually moving forward with changes in their instruction.

Virginia Beach Public Schools has worked hard to align their district's professional learning initiatives. The leadership team crafted a strategic framework—they named it the Compass to 2020, and it includes four goals for the entire division: high academic expectations, multiple pathways, social-emotional development, and culture of growth and excellence. All of the districtwide professional learning in Virginia Beach is aligned to the goals, as are the monthly literacy leader meetings. Individual schools are required to have a plan for continuous improvement that outlines their specific path toward achieving the goals set in Compass to 2020.

The central office of Teaching and Learning has a framework that guides the conversations around instruction that is connected to the division goals and their beliefs around transformational learning. This year, they focused on reading conferences. They connected independent reading and conferring with Goals 1 and 2:

**Goal 1 High Academic Expectations:** All students will be challenged and supported to achieve a high standard of academic performance and growth; gaps between these expectations and the realities for our student subgroups will be addressed.

**Goal 2 Multiple Pathways:** All students will experience personalized learning opportunities to prepare them for postsecondary education, employment, or military service.

The first step the team took to support this work was to revise their suggested daily minutes to identify a specific time dedicated to independent reading and conferring (not embedded in small group rotations as a task, which is where it was currently living in most schools). The Teaching and Learning team shared this change through a mandatory recorded webinar that all elementary teachers were required to complete. They also shared it in an "update" session at the annual summer administrators' conference in July as well as at the mandatory back-to-school literacy leader meeting in August.

The Teaching and Learning team knew that they had to build capacity around conferring since using this structure in reading was not a common practice. To address this, they added some information on conferring structures to their English/Language Arts front matter documents. Then, the team offered another professional learning session at their summer administrator retreat that was focused on conferring and strategy groups.

At their August Literacy Leader meeting, the Teaching and Learning team shared the front matter updates and gave the Literacy Leaders time to reflect on the changes. They asked the Literacy Leaders to submit exit ticket information to help them plan for future additional support. When they reviewed the exit ticket data, the team learned that that they should revisit and offer the summer conference session again since not many educators were able to attend the summer session.

The team then spent the time to develop a train-the-trainer version of the session on conferring and offered it to their Literacy Leaders. After experiencing the workshop, the Literacy Leaders began partnering with one another to share the presentation in individual buildings. In some Virginia Beach schools, conferring was already a priority and listed in their plan for continuous improvement as a strategy to address reading engagement and stamina and to increase reading achievement. The strategy of conferring was always connected to the Compass to 2020 goals of high academic expectations through multiple pathways. The Teaching and Learning team supported these schools by providing professional learning opportunities on conferring during their weekly collaborations, offering feedback, and conducting learning walks with leadership teams.

Finally, the team also offered a literacy academy to interested teachers focused specifically on independent reading and conferring. The literacy academies are a hybrid professional learning model that include four hours of face-to-face study and six hours of job-embedded practical application work.

Virginia Beach addressed the Compass to 2020 goals at the district level, at the school level, and also with individual teachers who self-selected the academy. An important aspect of this connected thread is "keeping the main thing the main thing" over time. Michael Fullan (Fullan et al., 2015) reminds us "When the school is organized to focus on a small number of shared goals, and when professional learning is targeted to those goals, and is a collective enterprise, the evidence is overwhelming that teachers can do dramatically better by way of student achievement" (p. 15). That connected thread—from the office of the superintendent to the language arts curriculum team to the building principal and finally into the classroom—is the important aspect of professional learning that eventually impacts student achievement.

## COLLABORATION

A critical component of all learning is collaboration. Collective learning is distinctive in that it challenges the traditional paradigm of isolationism that is pervasive in school culture. As discussed in Chapter 1, professional development is not the same as professional learning. For professional learning to truly occur, "the work of teachers must be embedded in a culture of learning" (Fullan et al., 2015). It is through that "culture of learning" where collaboration thrives.

*Change strategies often fail to recognize the power of a group and instead focus on an individual as the agent of change. Collaboration begins to harness the power of the group and uses the group to change the group.*

Hattie (2009) identified the high-impact teaching practices that we know teachers need to embrace as part of their practice. But those high-impact practices need collaboration. Hattie added that "establishing safe environments for teachers to critique, question, and support other teachers to reach these goals have the most effect on student outcomes" (p. 83).

Collaboration can take many forms—from partnerships, grade-level teams, or schoolwide endeavors to other professionals outside of the school or district. Collaborations across all of these configurations have been shown to support teacher change and student achievement (Allen, Pianta, Gregory, Mikami, & Lun, 2011; Johnson & Fargo, 2010, 2014; Meissel, Parr, & Timperley, 2016), however, when larger groups (such as whole grade levels or school buildings) collaborate, there is a greater chance of impacting change beyond a single classroom. Collaboration and coherence go hand in hand. When there is a trusting environment where all stakeholders have a common vision of the innovation being attempted and where actualizing that common vision is a collective effort, teachers' practice improves.

> *It is the culture of learning that is created through collaboration and coherence that truly promotes professional learning.*

It is the culture of learning that is created through collaboration and coherence that truly promotes professional learning. For example, it is difficult for less skilled teachers to enter a highly collaborative school with a strong culture of learning without improving their practice. It is often the absence of coherence and collaboration when professional learning does not have much effect (Fullan et al., 2015).

P. K. Yonge Developmental Research School, a laboratory school affiliated with the University of Florida, has made collaboration an integral part of their everyday experience—they went so far as to build a new school building with collaboration at its heart. Students and teachers are organized into multigrade learning communities and are housed in spaces that have transparent walls and a collaborative teacher space called a "fishbowl." Their space and the ways in which they have organized student groupings allow for significant collaboration among teachers and students. One of their professional learning structures, called Learning Community (LC) Meetings, allows for teachers to come together twice a month to discuss issues of teaching and learning. The LC leader (a teacher within the community who has been designated with coaching responsibilities) leads the meetings over the course of the school year to respond to the needs of the teachers to collaborate at high levels. For example, because the teachers often share responsibility for the achievement of students outside of their homeroom classes, they must come together to share observations and data collected related to student achievement. Consider the following interactions from one of their LC meetings.

**Jill** (LC leader): Let's talk about the progress of our small reading groups. You guys have the data from the last mastery tests. What are you noticing about how the students are progressing?

**Anjum:** My group that is in Set 1 has a distinct pattern. There are two out of the six kids that are clearly ready to move at a faster pace. I'm not able to accommodate them within my grouping. I've noticed that they are having a much easier time than the others in acquiring sight word knowledge. I think this is because they are finding success with reading and are more interested in reading, so they are spending more time with books.

**Michele:** Well, my kids that are in Set 1 have the opposite issue. The data shows that I have five out the seven who are ready to move faster, so I'm thinking that we regroup these kids, and you take the group ready to move faster, and I'll take the ones that are moving at a steadier pace. Will that work for you?

**Anjum:** Sure, but what are you noticing about the kids who aren't moving as fast? I want to make sure that I'm addressing their needs.

**Michele:** Well, it seems like the kids who are not steadily progressing are taking more time to learn sight words but also are having a harder time blending the individual sounds into words.

**Anjum:** So, do you think that I would need to increase the number of practice words we do?

**Michele:** Yes, but I also think they need more practice in connected text that uses those sounds to make up words.

**Anjum:** Ok. I can do that.

**Jill:** So, does anyone else have a similar pattern? How else might we need to regroup?

While this might on the surface look like a regular meeting of grade-level teachers, what's powerful about this interaction is the collective responsibility that the teachers have for all the students and how their teaching experiences support the learning they need to address student learning. If the teachers were responsible for just their own core group of students, they would not have the ability to share their learning or learn from the experiences of others. The meeting described above happens four to six times per year and not only shows the power of collaboration but also how experiences that happen over time support deep learning.

# DURATION

The duration of the professional learning experience is integral to the participants' learning. Just as students take time to acquire new knowledge and skills, so do teachers. While research has not defined a specific length of time that supports both teacher learning and student achievement, we know that professional learning must be "ongoing" and "of sufficient duration" (Ball & Cohen, 1999; Darling-Hammond, Wei, Andree, Richardson, & Orphanos, 2009; Desimone, 2009). None of the professional learning initiatives referenced in this text or other major reviews of professional learning research (Darling-Hammond et al., 2017; Darling-Hammond et al., 2009) were single events.

The effectiveness and importance of duration is dependent on the quality, design, and focus of the content and activities that comprise the professional learning effort. Due to a myriad of factors (e.g., change in staff, new directives from school boards, state mandates, etc.), it is extremely challenging for districts to maintain a consistent focus over time. Let's take a look at a large district in the southeast that managed to create a continuous improvement professional learning structure for their district that enabled a sustained focus for their approximately 176 K-12 schools.

Charlotte Mecklenburg Schools (CMS) is the second largest public school district in North Carolina with approximately 145,000 students. At the time, CMS was made up of ten learning communities—each led by a learning community superintendent. Organizing their learning communities in this way allows for efficiencies in oversight and support. It also allows for more effective collaboration and learning with a smaller number of educators in like roles.

CMS has worked diligently to offer professional learning opportunities for teachers and leaders that is focused on continuous improvement, ensuring learning is both ongoing and sustained over time. In order to facilitate this within the confines of such a large district, the administration developed instructional leadership teams (ILT). ILTs are comprised of a building principal, facilitator, and several teacher leaders. Each learning community attends one day during each of the five or so "ILT weeks" throughout the school year. The leadership teams in the learning communities and the central office staff work collaboratively to facilitate a rich day of content and leadership learning for the teachers and leaders that is focused on continuous improvement.

The district's goal for this work is that by the end of three years, all students will be able to write with evidence in response to complex informational text. Equally important is the district's goal to model continuous improvement professional learning experiences for teachers and leaders so that they in turn can carry the strategies and "leadership moves" back to their buildings and become leaders in their own right. They strive to develop instructional leaders by creating opportunities for strong teachers to take ownership of aspects of the schoolwide leadership and literacy practices, while also facilitating professional learning among colleagues.

In 2014, the district crafted a Strategic Plan titled Teaching Our Way to the Top. The first line of this plan reads, "The classroom of the future will be a place of learning without limits." One area of focus they established was around effective teaching and leadership. The curriculum office developed a plan through the use of their ILTs. They began by simply establishing goals for each of the three years.

**Goal Year One:**

- All students, independently, will use close reading strategies to comprehend complex informational text.

**Goal Year Two:**

- All students will use complex information text for rigorous discussions and use tools to organize their thinking to prepare for writing in response to the text.

**Goal Year Three:**

- All students will be able to write with evidence in response to complex informational text.

Then, they designed a continuous improvement model with rich days of learning facilitated by central office staff, principals, and teachers that were designed to push thinking around close reading, text dependent questions, academic conversations, prewriting, and writing. They asked ILTs to incorporate the work within their school improvement plans, practice the leadership moves by embedding the work in their buildings, and facilitate the learning with their own staff. Not only was the professional learning focused and sustained, but over time, this continuous learning process was one vehicle for keeping the entire staff of a very large school system focused on a similar goal.

Duration (as well as collaboration and coherence) is evident in the CMS ILT model. Sustaining a single focus over time and across content is challenging for many districts, however, through perseverance and teamwork, CMS was able to stay the course and effectively accomplish the goals for all three years of their ILT continuous improvement work. It is important to remember that while each of the elements described in this chapter has implications for quality professional learning, none can stand alone.

In each of the vignettes presented, you can see many elements coming together to create the learning experience. Because these elements are interrelated and interdependent, it is critically important that each of them be considered as you plan. The chart below is intended to help consider the elements presented in this chapter, but it is not intended to be used as a "checklist." There may be some experiences that are heavy on one element and less so on others. This is typical, and we should consider how the experiences, taken collectively, address the elements.

## EFFECTIVE ELEMENTS OF PROFESSIONAL LEARNING (APPENDIX 3)

| ELEMENT | HOW IS THIS ELEMENT ADDRESSED IN THIS LEARNING EXPERIENCE(S)? | HOW IS THIS ELEMENT INTERACTING WITH THE OTHER ELEMENTS TO SUPPORT STRONG PROFESSIONAL LEARNING? |
|---|---|---|
| **Active Learning** <br> • Are teachers directly engaged in constructing knowledge? (discussions, observations, etc.) <br> • Are they applying newly learned skills? <br> • Are the activities they engage in similar to the ones we might offer to students in classrooms? | | How does active learning interact with… Coherence? Collaboration? Duration? |
| **Coherence** <br> • Are the goals of the professional learning aligned or congruent with district and school goals? | | How does coherence interact with… Active Learning? Collaboration? Duration? |
| **Collaboration** <br> • Partnerships? <br> • Grade-level teams? <br> • Schoolwide endeavors? | | How does collaboration interact with… Active Learning? Coherence? Duration? |
| **Duration** <br> • Is the professional learning ongoing? | | How does duration interact with… Active Learning? Coherence? Collaboration? |

The four elements of effective professional learning cannot be viewed in isolation. In fact, we often found describing the elements as discrete characteristics difficult when writing. However, it is important that we, as leaders of learning, keep these constructs (active learning, coherence, collaboration, and duration) in the forefront of our minds when planning opportunities to support teacher growth and change. These elements are critical when planning both large-scale district-level professional learning plans and smaller building level plans. In the next chapter, we will explore the structures that support the integration of many of these elements into cohesive experiences for teachers.

## Questions for Reflection

- How might you consider the role of active learning, coherence, collaboration, and duration when planning professional learning in the setting in which you work?

- How will you consider the interconnectedness and supportive nature of the attributes when planning?

- How might you use the Effective Elements of Professional Learning tool for considering a professional learning path?

# CHAPTER 4

# Learning Structures

For too long, seminars, conferences, and guest speakers have dominated opportunities for teachers to deepen their knowledge of their craft, yet teachers have been loud and clear about the ineffectiveness of such approaches (Wei, Darling-Hammond, & Adamson, 2010). Recent research has focused on professional learning communities (PLCs), instructional coaching, and teacher inquiry as powerful catalysts of teachers' professional learning. Additionally, teachers have now begun creating their own powerful networks to support professional learning through Facebook groups, Twitter, and other online mechanisms that support their own goals and desires. In this chapter, we will consider each of these mechanisms and how they work together to begin to form a professional learning system that has the potential to become an effective way of work within schools and districts.

> *We need new ways of shaping schools to be true learning centers, places where adults and children are well supported in their learning and development.*
>
> —Drago-Severson, 2009, p.13

## PROFESSIONAL LEARNING COMMUNITIES

Research has indicated that in order for sustained change to occur in curriculum and instruction, a shared understanding of the nature of the innovation and what it can accomplish is integral (Joyce, Showers, & Rolheiser-Bennett, 1987). PLCs are defined as " groups of teachers who meet regularly for the purpose of increasing their own learning and that of their students" (Lieberman & Miller, 2008, p. 2). PLCs provide a consistent and coherent structure that aligns with the elements of powerful professional learning for teachers. Much has been written about the power of PLCs and how to organize schools to support the development and work of a PLC (See Dana & Yendol-Hoppey, 2015; Dufour, Dufour, Eaker, Many, & Mattos, 2016). In this section, we will refrain from a deep description and instead help link the work of PLCs to the characteristics of powerful professional learning.

## ATTRIBUTES OF PLCS

There are distinct attributes that define a PLC from other collegial groups. First is the shift in focus from schools being centers of *teaching* to centers of *learning* (DuFour, Eaker, & DuFour, 2005). This shift toward schools being centers of learning is a fundamental change from the traditional view that schools are places where teachers teach, and it is up to the students to learn. PLCs have a driving mission to ensure that *all* students achieve at high levels and that it is up to educators to work together to problem solve issues and concerns related to student achievement. McLaughlin and Talbert (2001) were among the first to study PLCs and their connection to student achievement. They noted that the greatest gains in student achievement occurred in PLCs that focused on promoting teacher learning and linking that learning to student achievement. The weakest gains were noted in communities of teachers who enforced traditional notions of schooling such as tracking, grading on a curve, and where seniority among teachers is highly valued. What separates these communities of teachers is the time spent focused on student achievement and the vision that *all* students can learn.

*Engaging in "inquiry," where groups of teachers discuss problems and solutions relating to teaching and learning, is the essential mission of a PLC.*

A second attribute is the notion of collective learning. Collective learning combines the characteristics of collective participation and collaboration described in Chapter 2. Collective learning positions teachers as leaders of their own growth and development (Lieberman & Miller, 2008) and builds on the premise that "two (or more) heads are better than one." As teachers engage in PLCs that have a strong sense of collective learning, they are better equipped to tackle difficult problems together, rather than on their own.

This kind of collective work leads to better connections across disciplines, deeper understandings and appreciation of the work of others, and binds members of a PLC in shared set of ideas (Sergiovanni, 1994). In doing this kind of work, members of a PLC develop collective responsibility for student success and show evidence that "when groups, rather than individuals are seen as the main units for implementing curriculum, instruction and assessment, they facilitate development of shared purposes for student learning and collective responsibility to achieve it" (Newman & Wehlange, 1995, p. 37). An illustration of this kind of collective work is evident in the vignette shared about P. K. Yonge Developmental Research School in Chapter 3.

A third attribute of PLCs is shared leadership and vision. PLCs are effective when there is shared leadership and a notion of "we're all on the same team and working on the same goal: a better school" (Hoerr, 1996, p. 381). The notion of a principal as manager must morph into principal as "lead learner."

Kouzes and Posner (1996), in their extensive study of leadership, found no instances where great achievement was made without the "active involvement and support of many people" (p. 106).

> *Administrators, along with teachers, must delve into the work together wondering, investigating, and seeking solutions to complex problems. The notion of leaders as "heroes" must be dispelled and replaced with a collaborative approach.*

PLCs are effective when all members of the school community share a collective vision of the goals of school. As addressed in the first attribute, what sets a PLC apart from other structures is the belief that all students can achieve and that the ultimate goal of school is to ensure that achievement takes place (Louis & Kruse, 1995). In a PLC, members are encouraged to not only collectively develop the vision for the institution but to continually use that vision as a marker in making decisions about teaching and learning (Isaacson & Bamburg, 1992).

## INSTRUCTIONAL COACHING

In many ways, we can consider PLCs as an overarching, organizational structure for professional learning in schools. Instructional coaching is a complementary mechanism that promotes collaborative, collegial learning in a supportive environment.

> *Instructional coaches promote active learning by directly linking content knowledge to classroom practice.*

There are many different facilitative stances instructional coaches might take (consultative, collaborative, reflective, etc.), but most importantly, working with an instructional coach offers teachers and others a partner in learning (See Aguilar, 2013; Knight, 2007, 2011).

> *A coach is someone to learn with and from—a colleague with whom to explore new ideas, try them out in the classroom, and reflect on their success.*

Most often, instructional coaches are used to continue the learning that we receive from outside opportunities (Gallagher, Woodworth, & Arshan, 2017; Penuel, Fishman, Yamaguchi, & Gallagher, 2007; Wei, Darling-Hammond, Andree, Richardson, & Orphanos, 2009) and supports the duration of professional learning. In this way, coaches can support the follow-up and continuous aspect of the professional learning necessary for change to take root in our practice (Guskey, 2000;

Garet, Porter, Desimone, Birman, & Yoon, 2001). Instructional coaches are a bit like stagecoaches—assisting us in moving from where we are in practice to applying what we have learned in our current context.

Instructional coaches support the "connected thread" of professional learning in a district. As Elmore (2004) writes, instructional coaches have the capability to engage teachers in a learning process in the very environment that the change takes place—the setting in which they work.

If the district has written into their strategic plan that performance assessments in all content areas and all grade levels will be a goal for the following school year, then one important part of that professional learning puzzle is the work the instructional coach does with individuals or teams of teachers. Instructional coaches can not only engage in profound and thoughtful pedagogical conversations, they can also support job-embedded classroom practice. For a powerful example of side-by-side coaching, be sure to read the vignette in Chapter 2 about Lindsey and Beth's work together.

## TEACHER INQUIRY

Inquiry has been a part of the teacher education vernacular since Dewey (1933) suggested teachers engage in "reflective action." Inquiry is a formal process that goes beyond being reflective on practice. Inquiry engages participants in asking questions that are rooted in their practice and working to carefully and systematically study them (Cochran-Smith & Lytle, 1993). Inquiry can be a powerful part of a comprehensive professional learning system.

## INQUIRY AS A STANCE

*When inquiry has become a stance rather than a project, it allows for knowledge and practice to be interconnected and positions the teacher as learner.*

Inquiry has typically been used as a professional development offering, usually an option that teachers could choose as part of menu of activities. When inquiry is engaged in as an "option," it is seen as a project or something to do for a fixed period of time (Cochran-Smith & Lytle, 2001). While an inquiry project could be a beneficial event, it is not enough to make a lasting impact. Proponents of inquiry as a vehicle for professional learning describe taking an "inquiry stance," where questioning one's own practice becomes part of the fabric of the teacher's work (Cochran-Smith & Lytle, 2001; Dana & Yendol-Hoppey, 2009).

## INQUIRY AS PART OF A PLC

At the heart of inquiry is the belief that teachers learn best when they are at the center of their learning. Like a PLC, inquiry positions teachers as the expert. When inquiry is a stance, either at a teacher level or school level, a PLC can provide a vehicle for the cycle of inquiry to develop and reoccur. Dana and Yendol-Hoppey (2008) describe a model for professional learning through inquiry and PLCs. Their term, "inquiry oriented Professional Learning Communities," is defined as a group of teachers working together in a PLC who engage themselves in continuous cycles of inquiry. Considering the elements of a PLC, inquiry is a natural, effective, and complementary facet of professional learning.

Important pieces of the professional learning puzzle are the structures we have in place for educators to learn together. With whom do we do the learning, and how does it happen? How many opportunities will we have to delve deeply into this topic? How will the new learning support or change our current practice? Considering how to pull various learning experiences together to form a cohesive plan is essential if we want to grow understanding and change teacher practice.

## PROCESSES FOR PROFESSIONAL LEARNING— HOW DO WE DO THE LEARNING?

As you begin to synthesize the characteristics of powerful professional learning (content-based, active learning, collective participation, collaboration, duration, and alignment) and the mechanisms for professional learning (PLCs, instructional coaching, and teacher inquiry), a beginning framework for a cohesive plan may be emerging. Within that framework, there are structures that support the development of various experiences that may comprise a full professional learning plan. We suggest a few structures below, but there are many others that you will find useful. We can consider the learning structures categorized in two ways: initial and ongoing.

## WORKSHOPS

For lack of a better word, we are calling a gathering of teachers from across the district to explore a common topic a "workshop." We draw on this word from the Readers and Writers Workshop model, although we realize that many times "workshop" is used to describe the very one-shot professional development activities we seek to change. We consider workshops an opportunity to use outside materials (i.e., articles, videos, expert voices) around a common topic or theme in teaching and learning and to deepen teacher understanding.

Often workshops can be used to kick off the learning that may take place with a group of teachers over the next several months or years. For example, a group of intervention teachers may decide to explore the concept of dyslexia together. They might choose to begin this exploration with a workshop on the topic of dyslexia facilitated by one of their colleagues who just completed a master's degree in reading and took an entire course devoted to dyslexia—a knowledgeable other. From there, the year-long plan might involve instructional observations, book studies, resource exploration, —and so on—a wide variety of ways the teachers might dig into the same topic and connect that to their own classroom practice.

It is interesting to note that in a comprehensive analysis of the relationship between professional learning and student achievement, all of the studies that showed a positive relationship had a workshop or institute as part of the learning design (Guskey & Yoon, 2009). These workshops had opportunities for teachers to engage with conceptual inputs, practice new instructional techniques, and to consider their own contexts as they learned. This helps us understand the power of active learning and conceptual inputs and their relationship with the duration of the learning.

Workshops on important instructional topics are not necessarily effective and productive on their own as stand-alone opportunities. However, within the context of a more productive professional learning plan that lasts over time and involves a myriad of learning activities used to structure the learning, workshops offer thoughtful occasions for teachers to gather together and explore the same concept. Please see Sarah's vignette in Chapter 2 about a full-day professional learning workshop.

## Protocols for Initial Learning Experiences

Let's start at the beginning—teambuilders, or ice breakers, at the beginning of your professional learning time with educators offer the opportunity to both establish camaraderie and build relationships. We want to quickly make participants feel comfortable talking, and most importantly, collaborating. In Chapter 3, we discussed the importance of teacher collaboration within the professional learning context so it is imperative that early on participants begin to feel safe sharing and taking risks with one another. To this end, using team builders to grow the sense of community is important at the very beginning of the work.

A team builder can be something as simple as an open-ended question that sets the stage for the work. The following are some examples:

- What was your favorite childhood book, and why?

- What after school activities did you participate in during high school?

- Who are the people in your family?

- What do you hope to accomplish this summer?

- What books are on your bedside table?

Team builders can also be more elaborate and involve more structure than these simple open-ended questions. When choosing a team builder for your audience, it is important to be mindful of both your participants' experience and their knowledge of one another. Team members who have been working together for a long time can participate in a more involved activity that might require more risk-taking, while members who are new to one another will appreciate a less complicated structure that involves sharing about themselves in a simpler fashion. In addition, it is always helpful to consider tying the team builder into the topic of the meeting.

We have included several examples of team builders in the appendix. One example is a Four Corners (Appendix 4) activity that we often use at the beginning of our work together. In this team builder each corner of the room represents a different like or dislike, such as book, author, or quote. Participants then select a corner and are offered the opportunity to connect with others who think like they do. This team builder offers participants the chance to connect with others who think like they do around personal likes and dislikes and is a fun way to get conversations started. Another example is the Compass Points (Appendix 5) activity —a great choice if you will be spending some time working together to accomplish a project or a task. Compass Points is an activity that supports learners in thinking about their own learning and working style and how it mirrors or compliments their teammates' styles. Including team builders in most of your professional learning experiences will help your participants better understand one another's strengths, weaknesses, and interests. Understanding their colleagues better, will help them more easily accomplish other learning tasks.

As you begin to engage in collaborative work with teams who will be working together over a duration of time, setting norms for the hard work ahead is critical.

> Effective teams generally have a set of norms or guidelines that govern individual behavior. Engaging in the initial process alone offers group members a glimpse into what might be helpful as they are working together.

Then, taking the time to follow up and reflect on the norms, how they are working and what might need to be edited, constantly brings to the forefront of the group members the importance of their collaboration with one another.

The following vignette illustrates the central role of norm setting and specifically the importance of all voices being shared and heard.

Last summer, Heidi was asked to facilitate norm setting for a team of instructional coaches. They work together in a network to coach several buildings. The nature of their work requires that they stay connected and collaborate. Many times, they even work together in partnership to coach one individual teacher—in this context it is critical that they operate as a team!

Heidi arrived at the school where instructional coaches were meeting and was ushered into the library where they were already working on an activity from the morning. As they finished up, Heidi went around the room and said "hello" and introduced herself to the team. When it was time to begin, she started by setting intentions for their time together—what were they excited to learn more about? Some were excited about growing their team, and some were excited to learn more about the norm-setting process.

Then, the coaches did some visualizing. They imagined planning with their teammates and having several ideas about how to approach a coaching conversation. They imagined what it might feel like to plan a session together, then be the one to facilitate and have it not go so well. They also imagined having an idea about a problem in a school setting that was different from what everyone else thought.

Heidi supported them in digging deep into how they wanted to interact with their teammates, how they wanted to be supported, and how they wanted their ideas to be received. They worked to craft "We will …" statements—exploring how they as individuals would contribute to a feeling of safety and community on their team.

During this process, the team spent a lot of time discussing the meaning of the word "remarkable." They were using the word "remarkable" to describe the coaching conversations they hoped to have throughout the year. Most of the coaches believed that "remarkable" implied that the conversations were rich and thoughtful. However, a few worried that "remarkable" might imply something to take note of that was not necessarily positive—and they were brave enough to share their concerns. The community these instructional coaches lived and worked in had experienced a White supremacist rally that summer that resulted in violence and ultimately the death of a community member. The event that transpired in the community was "remarkable" also, but the word had a very different meaning in this context. The debate and conversation around what the word "remarkable" meant was a terrific opportunity for Heidi and the team of coaches to practice their norms of asking honest questions and pushing to purpose.

Through this norm setting process, the instructional coaches realized and honored the importance of vocabulary, and the brave coaches who pushed back realized the importance of sharing their thinking, especially when it was something different than what the rest of the group was thinking! In the appendix, you will find an example of a protocol designed to support teams in their norm setting efforts (see Appendix 6).

*Finding ways to create space for everyone's voice to be heard is as important for adults as it is for students.*

Once the groundwork has been laid for open communication with the team of learners, you will want to develop a plan for ongoing learning—a plan for brief conversations, longer explorations of a topic, and classroom embedded learning experiences.

## PROTOCOLS FOR ONGOING LEARNING

Of course, there are many places to look for protocols to support the learning conversations you would like to have with your teams/teachers. Protocols can support conversations around disagreements, agreements, brainstorming, and so on. One place we often look is the National School Reform Faculty (www.nsrfharmony.org).

A simple protocol that supports collaboration and active learning through brainstorming content around a particular topic is a Chalk Talk (see Appendix 7). Chalk Talk is a protocol that allows the participants to share their thinking through a silent written brainstorming session. Take a moment, and consider Karen's experience facilitating her elementary school's beginning-of-the-year faculty meeting with a Chalk Talk.

It was preservice week, and Karen, a principal of an elementary school, walked into her first faculty meeting designed to get her teachers thinking about the bigger picture—curriculum, instruction, and assessment. In Karen's district, teachers are charged with incorporating Costa and Kallick's Learning and Leading with Habits of Mind (2008) (persisting, listening with understanding and empathy, thinking flexibly, striving for accuracy, etc.) into their daily instruction.

The problem Karen's school faced is that there are a lot of Habits, and they are just simply hard for student and teachers to remember. Karen's school's goal this year was to be more intentional around the Habits of Mind for both the teachers as well as for the students—they wanted to be sure to use and reflect on them in their daily work. For instance, she wondered, might the Habits serve as the research theme in some of their lesson study cycles?

Karen began by asking the participants to come close to a big white piece of butcher paper that she had taped on the library wall. She had already written all of the 16 Habits of Mind across the top of the butcher paper. Karen asked her staff not to talk and explained that their task was to write all of the units and activities they engaged in to support the Habits of Mind. The butcher paper began to fill up with different colored writing. Teachers were quiet in voice yet prolific in writing—adding many details of the different units and activities they taught that exemplified or connected somehow to the Habits of Mind. Slowly, the teachers began drawing arrows to connect their thinking. They all wrote in different colors and connected initial thoughts—so that it was very evident what the initial comment was and then how it was extended later by another participant.

The power of pushing each other's thinking through writing was amazing and unexpected! Her teachers connected ideas, added to one another's thoughts, and found similarities. Karen realized that not only did her teachers address the Habits of Mind in big units (e.g., through their expository nonfiction unit) but in small ways every day (e.g., through turn to your partner activities).

Offering her team a focused way of reflecting and writing helped to clarify members' individual thinking as well as their collective thinking. Karen was able to capture this all on the butcher block paper, and she in turn hung this in the faculty lunchroom. She made professional learning plans for the rest of the school year aligned to the *Habits of Mind* using their Chalk Talk as the impetus.

Another way to support educators discussing big instructional ideas and to offer some conceptual inputs to push their thinking is through the use of Quote Cards. Selecting quotes from several different well-known published authors who have written about their perspectives on the same topic and then discussing the topics through these lenses broadens our perspective on instructional issues. Sharing the author's writing allows for more knowledgeable others to inform our thinking—without going to the trouble of inviting several experts to speak at your event. You might also choose to use quotes from the same article or book as a way to help learners explore the entire resource (and one scholar's ideas) without actually reading the entire piece. There is a brief protocol in the appendix (see Appendix 8) that will support your use of the Quote Cards as a learning structure.

Aligning and situating the professional learning work within our own context is key. Creating situations and offering structures in which participants have the chance to discuss and solve problems with one another not only helps participants discover solutions to complex issues they are facing as teammates, it also helps to build a strong sense of community through engaging in rigorous, hard work together. Consider this vignette from a district struggling to come to grips with change in their teachers' instructional practice. They used a Philosophical Chairs (see Appendix 9) protocol to support their processing of different opinions.

Many years ago, Joanne, an elementary curriculum coordinator, had the chance to participate in a Philosophical Chairs experience with her instructional leadership team. She arrived at the meeting space in their district office, and her assistant superintendent, Ray, had posted the following statement on the whiteboard: "The role of a teacher is to design and guide students through engaging learning opportunities." She noticed two rows of chairs facing one another. Ray explained that one side was for participants who agreed with the statement. The other row of chairs was for staff who disagreed with the statement.

Ray knew that the teachers in his district were struggling with their role—they were a pretty traditional group and had been teaching in the county for a long time. Many believed that they were the experts in their content area, and that was the position they chose to take in their classrooms. Ray hoped to push the thinking of his instructional team and help them articulate why the role of the teacher was more facilitative. To this end, he gave them some quiet time to reflect on their thinking and whether or not they agreed or disagreed. Everyone was quiet and thoughtful. Then, Ray asked them to move and sit on one row of chairs or the other, depending upon their beliefs. Joanne looked around at her colleagues—curious about where they would sit and wondering if there was a "right" answer or not.

During the activity, they had the chance to defend their thinking about the role of a teacher. Some of them even switched sides several times. Ray explained that they had three rules as they engaged in the protocol—one person speaks at a time, everyone must have a turn before someone speaks twice, and they must repeat what the person on the opposing side said before sharing their opinion. As he facilitated the experience, Joanne was not only surprised by some of the positions her colleagues were taking but was also better able to see all sides of the issue due to the wisdom of some of her colleagues.

As we describe in Chapter 2, unpacking the why is important, and this protocol offers a vehicle for accomplishing this. Not only did Joanne leave with a better understanding of the topic, she also had a better understanding of her colleagues and their perspectives. Allowing space for disagreement and productive time to listen to others not only helps us understand complex professional issues in more thoughtful ways, it also helps colleagues develop empathy for one another and for different perspectives.

Another tool to help participants explore specific issues they are struggling with as individuals is the Consultancy Protocol (see Appendix 10). This is a great resource to use whenever you want to ground the conversation in our daily work and give teachers the chance to share their thinking around problems they are facing in their current classrooms. Individuals can share a dilemma they face and have the opportunity to receive feedback from their team about different instructional strategies they might try. Consider Cyndi, Jen, Paula, and Erin's use of the Consultancy Protocol. They serve as elementary instructional coaches in a medium-sized district. They meet once a week as a PLC to discuss their coaching roles and brainstorm strategies to support one another. Once a month, they use the Consultancy Protocol in order to offer one another concrete and specific feedback on particular coaching struggles.

Last week, it was Erin's turn to share her coaching dilemma. Erin shared that the third-grade team at Aldridge Elementary had asked her to help them think through their struggles with behavior—this class of Grade 3 students seemed particularly challenging and needy. They were often talking out of turn and made it difficult for the teachers to cover all that they needed to cover before the state assessment next month. Erin struggled with her role as a coach because after being in their classrooms it was very clear that the teachers were doing their best to cover content but were not taking the time to engage students in interesting activities that offered them choice in their learning. Finally, after telling her story, Erin shared her specific question: "How do I help this team see that it is less about managing the children's behavior and more about lesson design?"

The rest of the team asked a series of clarifying questions:

- How long have the teachers been teaching?

- Have you been in all of their classrooms?

- Were you able to offer feedback after observing?

- What is the academic achievement like of the students?

Then, they asked a couple of probing questions:

- Are there one or two teachers who might serve as examples or role models because things are going well in their classrooms?

- Do you think the teachers have a reason to be concerned about test scores?

Erin then restated her initial question: "How do I help this team value engaged learning more than test scores?" Cyndi, Jen, and Paula then participated in a rich conversation about supporting the third-grade team at Aldridge Elementary. Erin listened intently and took many notes so that she could reflect on their suggestions later. She shared later that she wanted to position the team leader as a model and invite the other teachers into her classroom to see her teach. She also wanted to explore a conversation with the reading specialist at the building to see about encouraging the administrative team to not discuss or expect test preparation until closer to the actual state test. Erin left the Consultancy Protocol conversation feeling well supported by her team. She had a list of coaching strategies that she wanted to try to better support the Grade 3 team at Aldridge Elementary and the hope that she could support them in becoming more effective teachers.

As we can see from this vignette, not only did Erin leave the meeting excited about new ideas to try, but Cyndi, Jen, and Paula all learned from the conversation as well. They had many similar situations in their own coaching of teams of teachers and were thus able to extrapolate from the conversation to their own dilemmas. Digging into articles and having conversations using text rendering protocols is another very effective way to structure the learning so the teachers collaborate and think together. Text rendering protocols offer the chance for learners to agree with or argue with one another safely about important instructional ideas and research in their reading. Taking the time to read a research article and then have conversations about what they just read provides adults with multiple opportunities to make sense of their learning in collaborative teams. An example of a protocol that supports this kind of conversation is the Final Word protocol that can be found in Appendix 11.

Another way to use articles or books in your professional learning offerings is through offering book studies on popular professional books. There are many ways to structure the study of a professional book. Read on to learn about how Carol organized a book study for her teachers.

Carol was a world language leader in a medium-size district that was moving toward one-to-one implementation, in which each student is given a digital device. To help facilitate that, she hosted a semester-long book club with a group of middle school language teachers. The group read a professional book and discussed foreign language instruction using digital tools. Carol used the work of David Thornburg to help organize their study. Thornburg identified three archetypal spaces for learning—the campfire, the watering hole, and the cave (Davis & Kappler-Hewitt, 2013). The campfire is a space where people gather together to learn from an expert or in a large group. The watering hole is an informal space where peers can share information and discoveries. The cave is a private space where an individual can think and reflect. The following page shows the plan that Carol designed to support their work over the course of four meetings.

**Session I:**

- **Icebreaker:** Who are you (name and role), and why are you here?

- **Cave time:** Respond to a Google doc that is populated with digital tools. Answer this question: How well do you know these tools, and which ones do you want to learn more about?

- **Watering hole:** Using a T column chart, on one side write the digital tools that you use currently in your classroom. On the other side write the learning outcomes you hope will occur based on the use of these tools.

- **Campfire:** Share the T column chart with the group. Then, respond to this question: How do you connect language instruction with technology?

**Session II:**

- **Icebreaker:** What's new since the last time we gathered?

- **Cave time:** Skim through Chapters 1, 2, 3, 4, 7, and 8. What are the important takeaways for you and the burning questions you still have?

- **Watering hole:** In small group of 4, discuss your important takeaways.

- **Campfire:** Share any important burning questions and next steps.

**Session III:**

- **Icebreaker:** How do you use digital resources to support your own work?

- **Cave time:** Take a moment to watch these videos on virtual foreign language instruction. Be sure to use your headphones.

- **Watering hole:** Discuss the following questions in small groups:

  1. What do we know about learning a second language?

  2. How does what we know about learning language inform video and audio storytelling?

3. What do we want to remember as we make plans to teach our students video/audio storytelling?

4. Create a chart to share with the whole group.

- **Campfire:** Share your chart with the whole group.

**Session IV:**

- **Icebreaker:** What digital strategy have you tried since we last met?

- **Cave time:** Create two Google documents titled as follows:

  ○ Tools I am Interested in Using

  ○ Lessons Learned from Virtual Language Instruction

- **Watering hole:** Share your documents in your small group.

- **Campfire:** Because this is our last meeting, share your future plans: 5-5-5—What I plan to do in 5 days, 5 weeks, 5 months.

Using a book to guide conversation over time with a team helps educators to think collaboratively about new ideas, actively try them out in classrooms, and then reflect on their success. Carol also connected their study of digital tools to the district's bigger focus of one-to-one instruction. The alignment between the district's goals and Carol's goals was evident to the teachers and made their learning much more productive. A protocol for using the Archetypal Spaces for Learning can be found in Appendix 12

Teachers often appreciate professional learning that is closest to the classroom and truly job embedded. We can learn the most from simple opportunities to experience a lesson and then talk about our experience with our colleagues— exploring what worked for students in the lesson and what activities were not successful. Sometimes, we can accomplish this same goal through watching videotaped lessons. Keri, an instructional specialist with the district, has had the opportunity to facilitate lesson study in many buildings. This past fall, she worked with some teachers to prepare for a model lesson experience using real students in real classrooms. The prework they did together to set the stage helped make the observation a much richer learning experience for the primary teachers.

Keri began her small group session by asking the teachers to share their teaching and learning challenges. Without pause, Vivian, a second-grade teacher, eagerly raised her hand and blurted out with frustration, "It is October, and my students aren't writing enough. They barely write two sentences in 15 minutes. I need more volume out of them, and I don't have any extra minutes in the day to give for writing time!" It was clear Vivian had been losing sleep over her students' lack of stamina. The rest of Vivian's K–2 team were visibly nodding their heads in agreement. Carol, the more experienced teacher in the group, even said a quiet, "Amen." At this point in the conversation, Keri could have given the group a list of possible reasons for this behavior and an accompanying list of solutions. She fought this urge and dug a bit deeper into their dilemma by asking open-ended questions. Keri asked, "What does their writing behavior look like?"

Carol shared, "I notice lots of erasing the same word several times."

Rhonda also responded, "Many of my students are spending too much time copying a word from the wall or their personal dictionaries."

Vivian said sadly, "My kids just stare at their papers and don't write anything."

Keri's next open-ended question to the group was, "What might be some reasons for this challenging writing behavior? How might we help our students?"

Carol said, "I think it has to do with confidence, many of my student will only write words they are confident spelling."

Rhonda agreed, "Most of my students aren't risk-takers."

Vivian shared, "I think it is because they have very little experience as writers. They are taught to spell in isolation. They are tested on isolated lists of words but not explicitly taught how to integrate their spelling knowledge into their writing."

Keri thought for a moment and then said, "It sounds like the real challenge for our students might stem from the heart. So how might we help our students become brave spellers and approximate their spelling more frequently in order to increase the volume of writing?" The three teachers were silent. Keri sat on her hands and reminded herself that wait time is healthy. Still, they did not respond.

After a few minutes had passed, Rhonda hesitantly offered, "I think we need to model what "brave spelling" looks like."

Carol added, "I do this. We actually celebrate the brave words after writing time is over and chart them. My kids love to publicly share their hard work, especially LONG words. They like how their classmates respond with ooohs and ahhhs."

Vivian asked, "Can I come to your room later today to see your chart? You know, maybe it has to do with the tools we give them. My special education students have really responded well to keyboarding—maybe that can help increase stamina and volume?"

Keri followed up with more questions, "What might we do for students who are spending too much time using the word wall or their personal dictionaries?"

Rhonda thought for a moment and then replied, "I think my word wall is too small and hard for students to see, but I am required to have one in my room."

Vivian offered, "My students have a personal word wall in their writing folders. It's a manilla file folder that we add words to weekly."

Carol shared, "We bought premade personal dictionaries, but I think I need to teach my students how to use them more effectively."

As this conversation came to an end, Keri reflected on her observation that the group's suggestions were almost identical to her own and now she did not own the thinking for the group—they were able to determine solutions without Keri telling them the answers to their dilemmas. The next step was for Keri to intentionally integrate one of the suggestions into the demonstration lesson so that Carol, Rhonda, and Vivian could see their thinking come alive in the classroom. She gave them the following specific look-fors as they watched her teach a writing lesson to Vivian's students:

- What did you notice about the students' thinking and/or behavior?

- What techniques did I use to support student learning?

- What evidence do you have that students were increasing their writing stamina?

- What in the lesson planning allowed this to happen?

- What does this tell you about student thinking?

Having this conversation before the actual lesson experience set Vivian, Carol, and Rhonda up for rich learning. You will find a protocol for the conversation you might facilitate before a lesson experience in Appendix 13 titled, "Preparing for and Debriefing a Demonstration Lesson."

## Virtual Collaboration

Not all professional learning experiences can be face to face. A full professional learning plan is remiss without some attention to virtual collaboration and personalized learning networks. Virtual learning often can offer participants opportunities that are typically not as obvious when learning in a face-to-face setting. First, learning together virtually enables tremendous opportunity for accessibility. Teachers from all over the world can participate in learning experiences—geography is not a hindrance. This diverse participation often challenges the thinking of groups and informs practice in districts. If the goal of the professional learning is an increase in ideas and perspectives, virtual sessions often make this possible.

Second, participation increases—not only does geography not matter, teachers can also participate from the comfort of their homes. Childcare is not an issue, and the stress of being away from home is reduced. Participants can be on their sofa with the television on in the background and their children tucked in bed for the evening. Third, collaboration amongst learners is simpler—teachers from many different schools can work together on the same project. No longer is there a need for finding time and locations in which to meet to work on projects. Finally, there are many different digital tools that offer a wide variety of opportunities for reflection (e.g., blogs, videos, and podcasts).

There are a myriad of platforms for educators to connect virtually with one another. Districts often have their own internal platforms (Canvas, for instance) and technologies (Zoom, Google Hangouts, etc.) for allowing their staff to work with one another in both an asynchronous and synchronous setting. Many of the protocols and structures we have already shared and discussed can be used in similar ways through these virtual channels.

An important consideration to keep in mind when planning for virtual learning, just as when you are planning for face-to-face learning, are the four features of effective professional learning that we discussed in Chapter 3. Be sure to engage participants in *active learning* through virtual observations of lessons, discussions in small and large groups, time for planning, and even opportunities to practice. Ask whether the virtual learning experience has *coherence*? As we discussed, coherence with district and school goals and state and national reform efforts has an impact on both teacher learning and student achievement. A critical component of all learning—face to face or virtual—is *collaboration*. Offer opportunities for participants to collaborate with one another. Finally, *duration* is important in the virtual setting, also. While you might keep your sessions brief, you will want to be sure to build in learning experiences over time. To help you process these four essential components when planning for virtual learning, you might want to use our Reflecting on Effective Elements of Professional Learning tool found in Appendix 3.

Social media offers platforms to support virtual collaboration as well, and many districts are beginning to take advantage of this kind of learning. One process that districts often use and is helpful for processing big ideas across a variety of locations is a Twitter chat. Twitter chats allow for educators across districts to chat about important issues from the comfort of their own homes and couches. They can even multitask and still enjoy the collegiality of a Twitter chat. It is also a way to extend the conversation and invite knowledgeable others from all over the world to add their thinking. Here are some ideas to think about when you decide to organize a Twitter chat for your staff or district.

It is often helpful to have two moderators cofacilitate the conversation. One moderator can be responsible for posing the initial questions; the other moderator can probe to push the conversation deeper and retweet interesting comments. Many Twitter chat facilitators will have a transcript open in another document so that they can easily copy and paste into a Tweet as they are facilitating. The questions are often planned far in advance and added to the transcript, along with other links, images, and quotes that might be useful to the learners.

When facilitating a Twitter chat, consider the timing and frequency of the questions. You will want to allow enough time for participants to think, then answer, and finally comment on others' thinking. On the other hand, you want to be sure not to allow too much time to go by that you lose participants' interest. When determining topics and questions, do your best to keep them friendly, open ended, and engaging. The first question of your chat might elicit the definition of the topic. You will want at least one question to lead to pictures or resources. Your closing question can be one that makes participants feel connected and pleased that they have participated.

The following are the questions from a sample Twitter chat that Lori organized for her reading specialists at the beginning of the school year. The group was getting ready to embark on a year-long study of effective writing instruction. This chat was an initial team builder focused on exploring the reading specialists' personal writing processes.

**Q1:** Reflect on the steps you take when you write. What is the process you go through? What do you do first? Next?

**Q2:** What do you find helpful as a writer?

**Q3:** What are your struggles when writing? Are the same struggles true for your students?

**Q4:** Is your writing process different based on the kind of writing you are doing?

**Q5:** What digital tools do you use when you are writing? What digital tools do you use with your students?

**Q6:** Do you write to learn in your daily life? What does that look like?

**Q7:** Do you write with colleagues? What is that collaboration like? Is the same true for your students?

**Q8:** What would you like to continue to think about regarding your writing life?

By offering an initial Twitter Chat as a way to kick off their exploration of writing instruction, Lori was able to build a relaxed sense of community with her team. The questions she crafted helped her reading specialists focus on their own writing experiences and what their experiences might mean for their students. Offering the chat about their own experiences in an informal setting at night also helped her team feel engaged and comfortable with one another. You can find a planning guide for Twitter chats in Appendix 14.

## LEADING THE CHANGE

When we are able to design experiences that make space for long-term learning that aligns with school and district goals, teachers feel as though their learning matters. When that learning is collaborative and active, teachers better understand how to shift instruction to meet the needs of their particular students. And when all of these elements are attended to within the structures described in this chapter, teacher learning moves into the very fabric of our institutions. We are moving toward a professional learning system rather than a series of nonrelated events. Changing schools into learning institutions for both students and adults is our ultimate goal, and a comprehensive professional learning system supports the systemization of such learning.

New ways of leading professional learning are necessary to support deep learning for adults. The role of leaders has shifted significantly over the last ten years, and many school- and district-based leaders have taken on the role of designing professional learning. In the next chapter, we will focus on the role of the facilitator of professional learning and what competencies and dispositions support the changing landscape of professional learning.

# Questions for Reflection

- How do structures such as PLCs, coaching, and inquiry support the elements of learning (active learning, coherence, collaboration, and duration) that are discussed in Chapters 2 and 3?

- How might you consider planning for professional learning in your setting that includes some of the mechanisms we describe in Chapter 4?

- What might a long-term plan look like that uses the elements and mechanisms described?

# Notes

# CHAPTER 5

# Lead Learner

The role of the facilitator of professional learning is one that is crucial to the impact on teacher learning and student achievement. We call the facilitator of professional learning the "lead learner" to illustrate the stance necessary for continuous learning. This lead learner could be an instructional coach, a district supervisor, a principal, an assistant principal, a teacher leader, an external partner, or anyone reading this book! Whoever is leading the learning is the lead learner.

> *When one teaches, two learn.*
>
> —attributed to Robert Heinlein

We have all been a part of professional learning situations when the facilitator has positioned himself or herself as an "expert," and it was clear he or she wasn't, or it became painfully apparent that the facilitator didn't have the experience necessary to push the learning deeper. As we have explored throughout the first four chapters of this book, we know there are research-based elements that support powerful learning, however, it is not through checklists of elements that true learning occurs. It's through "creating learning situations where teachers and leaders learn together" (Fullan, Hord, & von Frank, 2015, p. 7). How might we rethink the stance of those leading the learning to truly model how our profession is as much about learning as it is about teaching?

A professional learning experience could be grounded in solid theory, have a clear content focus, be of significant duration, require collective participation, and have active learning opportunities built in, yet not have an impact on teacher or student learning due to the facilitator. Research suggests that the facilitator is "crucial to the success of the professional development program" (Schifter, Bastable, & Russell, 1999; Seago, Mumme, & Branca, 2004 p. 10). Similarly, research around instructional coaching, which draws on many of the same characteristics as facilitators, suggests that the interpersonal skills of a lead learner may play a more significant role than content or pedagogical knowledge (Knight, 2004). Expert support and coaching was found to be present in many of the professional learning studies that showed impact on teacher change and student achievement (Darling-Hammond, Hyler, & Gardner, 2017).

There are three important stances a lead learner must take in order for the learning to be successful:

- Communicate effectively the goals and intentions of the professional learning experience.

- Develop rapport and trust with and among those in the learning experience.

- Reframe the discourse and adjust the activities to respond to the idiosyncratic needs of particular teachers while still maintaining the goals of the professional learning experience

We see this effort reflected in many different learning situations, not just academic contexts. Bronco Mendenhall, the football coach at the University of Virginia in Charlottesville, reflecting on this same dichotomy, said in an interview in the Daily Progress:

> I'm anxious to help another group of young men win, I'm anxious to help them grow and develop.... And I'm anxious to develop relationships. And that comes with time.

He then looked at Peck and Kaufusi [two football players].

> Even though I'm the coach of these two, I don't feel like that. I feel like friends. And I'm hopeful I can develop that relationship as well.

Mendenhall is conscious of meeting the needs of the whole while at the same time building relationships with each individual player.

*Being responsive to the individual needs of the participants while remaining true to the needs of the whole group and the experience is one of the most challenging tasks a lead learner faces.*

So, how do we accomplish these lofty goals as lead learners? How do we "help another group" of educators with their learning goals while at the same time building relationships? What stance should effective facilitators of professional learning take? In order to make sure both happen, it is important to think about our work as facilitators within sessions as well as the planning that occurs before sessions. Let's start by discussing facilitation as a lead learner.

## FACILITATION

Our colleague, Peter Brunn, offers a list in his book, *The Lesson Planning Handbook* (2010) for teachers to consider as they facilitate student learning. While his list is designed for students, each of these has an implication for adult learners as well:

- **Listening fully** and learning how to be a better listener

- Presenting ways to craft and deliver **open-ended questions** that probe thinking

- Exploring the **effect of our words on the learning**

## LISTENING FULLY

We start by listening fully. In the words of Peter Senge (1994), "To listen fully means to pay close attention to what is being said beneath the words. You listen not only to the 'music,' but to the essence of the person speaking. You listen not only for what someone knows but for what he or she is" (p. 377). We so often think about listening fully in the context of our instruction with students, but we often don't spend enough time listening fully during our professional learning sessions with teachers and other adults. Brunn (2010) writes about "teaching on the edge of your seat" in order to be fully present with your students. This is just as true for adult learners as it is for children in our classrooms.

In order to listen fully, we must be completely prepared for and organized for the work. Spend time beforehand thinking about the needs of the groups of adults you will be supporting. Ask yourself some of the following questions:

- Who are the adults we are working with?

- What are they interested in and curious about?

- What are their pain points?

- What brings them joy?

- What resources do they have available?

- What are their past experiences?

Then, explore how the answers to these questions might inform or change your time with participants. Are there more participants than you originally thought? If so, might you need to address the environment and add more chairs or a microphone? Are the pain points due to unwanted curriculum changes? If so, you might need to build in time for the participants to grieve and problem solve. Are the resources in the district rich or limited? Does time need to be devoted to finding resources?

> *As facilitators, we must work hard to avoid the easy temptation of filling participants' heads with our knowledge or our perceived knowledge and instead allow space for participants to discover their own knowledge.*

In addition to preparing to listen fully, we must work to listen while we are in the moment. Often, facilitators of professional learning are tasked with "delivering" information, whether it is a new curricular innovation, teaching technique, or way of work. This form of delivery often leads to very passive learning on the part of the participants.

We (authors) both have struggled with attending to the needs of our participants versus accomplishing our learning goals, albeit in slightly different ways as shown in the following vignette.

**Marisa:** I remember just how long it took for me to prepare for workshops or learning sessions I was delivering. I would spend days and hours reading, preparing slides, and thinking about classroom examples and work samples to showcase. In all of this preparation, there was deep learning. When it came time to share that information with others, I was ill-equipped to do much more than just "tell" my stories, my examples, and my learning. What I failed to recognize at that time was that I needed to set up experiences for the professional learning participants that mirrored the learning I was doing while I was preparing for them. We know the saying—those who are doing the work are those who are doing the learning. What is interesting to consider is that this was a significant departure from the way I planned and implemented lessons for my students. I had lost track of myself as a teacher in my role as an adult learning facilitator.

**Isabel:** During my first couple of years teaching, I was given the opportunity to present at a Title 1 Conference. My session was about the power of "push-in" Title 1 programs rather than the traditional "pull-out" model. I was so excited about the work and came ready to share all the research out there on how ineffective traditional pull-out models were. The room was full of very experienced Title I teachers who had been implementing a pull-out model for years, and the research I shared only made them angry. I wasn't prepared for their frustration. Hindsight is 20/20, of course, and I know now that I failed to take into consideration who my audience was and what their pain points were. Had I attempted to get some information from my participants at the start of the session (or even spent time reflecting on who might be in the audience), I might have been able to address their frustration or worry more successfully.

## OPEN-ENDED QUESTIONS

When we are listening fully, we realize when we need to take a step back or push thinking forward. One way to consider pushing thinking is through open-ended questions and probing.

A consideration is that when we are situated in a familiar context, it is often difficult to really see beyond what is at the surface. That is where carefully crafted questions on the part of the facilitator take the learning deeper and might enable the facilitator to more closely meet the needs of the participants.

*We know that powerful professional learning consists of situating the learning within the participants' own context, whether that is through the use of observation, coaching, or student work samples.*

Consider the following questions that could be used when debriefing a video or observation of classroom practice:

- What did you notice about the students' thinking or behavior?

- What techniques did the teacher use to support student learning?

- What evidence do you have that the lesson goals were met?

- What in the lesson planning allowed _____ to happen?

- What did _____ tell you about student thinking?

Each of these questions allow for learners to consider many points of view and build upon each other's thinking. Through the use of questions such as these, facilitators have the opportunity to truly consider the direction to take the learning, decide where to probe further, and how to redirect thinking if necessary. These questions can be found on the protocol called Preparing for and Debriefing a Demonstration Lesson (Appendix 13).

Probing learners' thinking and making considerations for how to deepen their learning is somewhat of an art form. Very similar to a classroom situation, participants in professional learning often think there is a "right" answer.

*Through the use of open-ended questions, we begin to change the course of the learning and shift the tone from "a room of novices learning from an expert" to one in which all are learners.*

Consider the following responses to probe thinking:

- Say more about that.

- Why do you think that?

- How is your comment different than _____?

- What do others think?

Responses and probes support learners in deepening their knowledge beyond the surface-level responses that often bubble up immediately. At first, participants might not be used to such a learning environment. As a lead learner, building a community and creating a sense of trust are foundational to any subsequent rigorous work, hard conversations, or deep dives into content. Therefore, the language we use as facilitators is paramount.

## EFFECT OF OUR WORDS ON THE LEARNING

Many of us have been in learning contexts where we knew we were not safe to take a risk. Some facilitators are seen as such an expert that participants would never consider raising a different perspective. In some professional learning situations, there is a feeling of complacency in the room—everyone is just waiting for the session to be over. The language the facilitator uses in any learning session sets the tone for the learning that is going to take place. In order for the session to be productive, educators must feel like they are in a safe environment for taking risks and that all ideas are valued. One way facilitators can promote this environment is through the use of neutral responses. Take the following scenario as an example:

Ashley was facilitating a grade-level professional learning community meeting where the teachers were planning for an upcoming unit of instruction. The focus was on the comprehension strategy of visualizing.

**Ashley:** Let's take a minute to think about what visualizing does to help students in their comprehension of text. Who might start the conversation?

**Elizabeth:** Well, I think it's really about making mental images of what the author has written.

**Ashley:** Great! Who else?

**{Silence}**

**Ashley:** Ok. So now let's look through the lessons in the unit and talk about the texts chosen for visualization.

Now consider this alternative to the same scenario:

**Ashley:** Let's take a minute to think about what visualizing does to help students in their comprehension of text. Who might start the conversation?

**Elizabeth:** Well, I think it's really about making mental images of what the author has written.

**Ashley:** Thank you. What do others think?

**Michael:** I think it's about making mental images, but I also think it's really important to connect those images to the words the author has used.

**Ashley:** Say more about that, Michael.

**Michael:** Well, sometimes, when the kids draw mental images, they just draw really basic stuff and don't really consider the tone that the author is using or really think in a sophisticated way about the words. I think this is a place where we need to put some emphasis in this unit. They're in third grade now. Their mental images and visualizations should be deeper.

**Ashley:** Thank you. Who thinks something different than what Michael and Elizabeth have shared?

**Amanda:** I'm not sure that it's different, but I think visualizing really helps kids get the nuances that an author is trying to convey. For example, word choice. When an author chooses certain words, she means to convey certain images. I'm not sure that the kids always get that.

As the facilitator, Ashley posed the question about how the strategy of visualizing helps students comprehend text deeper. She wanted to ensure that the teachers had a baseline understanding of how the strategy works. In the first scenario, when Elizabeth offered her thinking, Ashley said "Great!" and the conversation ended. The teachers felt like the "right" answer had already been given. Although Ashley tried to open the conversation up for more responses, the teachers were not necessarily willing to engage further because it seemed as though the question had been answered. The second scenario really illustrates the power of not only neutral response (notice that Ashley simply responded with "thank you" to each person) but also probing for more information. The conversation in the second scenario really allowed the teachers to consider their teaching of visualizing at a much deeper level.

We have discussed the power and importance of building relationships with individual participants and the moves we make as facilitators to establish trust. Let's think about structuring the professional learning so that it addresses the needs of the whole group. Planning is key!

## PLANNING

When planning for professional learning, we must think deeply about our instructional needs and goals—both the big and often year-long picture as well as any shorter more specific learning sessions. In order to meet the needs of the whole group, consistently attending to our instructional goals is critical. Effective professional learning plans make time and space during the learning cycle to reflect on what the goals are and determine if the learning activities are supporting our work in accomplishing the goals. Thoughtful leaders help their teams to think deeply about where they are as a group in their learning and where they want to be after a year of learning together. Then, the learning is designed so that it addresses all of the goals.

Most importantly, spending time determining our initial question, topic, or goal before planning for the professional learning helps define what that learning looks like and ensures that our goals are met. During this planning time, meet with others to determine what it is they want and need to learn more about—creating a needs assessment—so that we can begin with the end in mind. It is important to ask, What data do we need to help make a decision about our professional learning goals? Is it student literacy assessment data? Do we need a teacher survey based on interest and perceived need? Should we also use our classroom walk through data to determine needs?

*Coherence between what we learn from our needs assessment and the professional learning opportunities is imperative. Once the goals are determined, then we discuss and refine them for the learning— thinking about both the content we are exploring and the participants' enthusiasm for the experience.*

One process tool that we have used to support both our big picture thinking for district level learning as well as coaching sessions with individual teachers is the Plan, Do, Study, Act model (or PDSA) developed by Walter Shewhart and Edward Deming (Moen & Norman, 2009). This learning cycle contains four continuous and recursive steps: plan, do, study, act—all designed to support constant reflection and the willingness to adopt or support ideas and practices that are either working or not working. The PDSA model is a simple but effective protocol for groups or individual learners to use to explore learning or change over time.

## PLAN

The first stage of the PDSA model involves intensive planning. During this phase, participants identify a goal or a purpose, formulate an idea, define what success might look like, and begin to put the plan into action. Of course, there are many topics a group might decide to explore. For example, is the goal to learn more about how to teach students to write persuasively? Perhaps as a group of literacy leaders in a district we want to support our teachers to think more deeply about how to effectively instruct students to write opinion pieces. To this end, during the planning phase of the PDSA cycle, we might draft a semester-long plan with six components that looks something like this:

1. An introductory face-to-face session on the power of argument writing and a sharing of professional resources on opinion writing.

2. An expectation that all teachers in our learning cohort will teach an opinion writing unit over the next several weeks.

3. A check-in virtual session in the middle of the unit to address any questions that teachers might have.

4. Another face-to-face session at the end of the unit to score individual student work with a common rubric.

5. A closing virtual session to debrief the experience of learning together.

6. A Google survey to better understand what the cohort group of teachers might need next.

As we begin to think more specifically about some of the specific sessions, we might reflect on the following questions:

- What are the participants interested in and curious about?

- What are their pain points? What brings them joy?

- How will you use the information you gather during the initial question to frame the conversations?

- How can you help participants see learning through their students' eyes?

- What research or professional reading might you provide that supports your approach and will help to build theoretical knowledge?

- How will you support you participants in a call to action at the conclusion of the PDSA cycle?

Once the plan is nailed down, begin to focus on the logistics. Decide who will do what and when and what your timeframe is.

## DO

Now it is time to actually carry out the plan. During the second stage of the PDSA model, the plan is implemented. Throughout this stage, take detailed observational notes and gather a wide variety of data to help determine if the strategies and activities are working to support both the collective and individual teacher learning.

## STUDY

The study phase of the model involves observing and learning from the consequences of our activities. Outcomes are explored and decisions are made about the plan's success or failure, or some combination of the two. We might ask ourselves questions about the experiences like the following:

- Was our instructional content rich enough?

- Did we meet the needs of both the group as a whole as well as the individual participants?

- Is the cohort still enthusiastic about the work? If not, how can we address this?

- What do the data from the student writing samples tell us?

- When we go back to our initial meeting brainstorm and goal setting to compare what we have done with what our initials goals were, what did we accomplish?

- What did we learn from our Google survey? What are our next steps?

## ACT

Once we have made sense of our learning, then we determine what modifications should be made to the plan. Now, we act on what we have learned. The act phase closes the recursive cycle and integrates the learning. We can adjust our goals, change our methods, brainstorm new ideas, or broaden the learning to a larger group. Based on the conversations, we determine next steps. Do we need to modify the plan for next year's new cohort of teachers? Do we need to do more—was a semester experience enough? If so, what might we do next based upon our data? What does this group want/need now? What might our next steps be? Are there more data we still need to collect?

The PDSA cycle can be repeated over and over again as part of a never-ending cycle of continuous learning and improvement. As the lead learners, it is imperative that we strive to see the big picture—what does this learning look like over the course of time?—before we think about the details and address the needs of the individual learning sessions. The PDSA model supports this thinking and pushes us toward reflection. We must think about both aspects of the learning, the big picture and the small details, in order for sustained growth to occur. Consider the following examples of the PDSA in action:

# PDSA Framework: Grades 2 and 3 Vocabulary Instruction Through Interactive Read Alouds

## PLAN

**Participants:**

- 3 elementary literacy specialists

- 6 lead teachers from Grades 2 and 3

- Central office coordinators

**Goal:** Explore students' vocabulary acquisition during whole group interactive reading lessons

**Timeline:** September-January

**Tasks:** Lesson study experiences using interactive read aloud lessons with an emphasis on vocabulary as well as comprehension.

## DO

Conduct three lesson study cycles (October, November, December) focused on vocabulary instruction within interactive read aloud lessons.

## STUDY

After reviewing the data from each cycle, we determined that we lacked a deep understanding of effective vocabulary instruction ourselves. The following important questions we explored:

- Did the students learn and use the words in the conversations or writing?

- Do we have a bank of strategies for teaching vocabulary that are effective?

## ACT

- Partner with the local university and offer several courses on literacy instruction to support elementary teacher knowledge.

- Explore different instructional programs for teaching vocabulary.

- Purchase several professional books on vocabulary acquisition and instruction for the literacy facilitators in the buildings to facilitate book groups.

# PDSA FRAMEWORK FOR AN INSTRUCTIONAL COACHING CYCLE

| |
|---|
| **PLAN** |
| **Participants:** |
| • MS instructional coach |
| • MS intervention teacher |
| **Goal:** How do we keep students on track and engaged during intervention instruction? |
| **Timeline:** February–March |
| **Tasks:** Lesson observations and feedback, instructional conversations between coach and teacher. |
| **DO** |
| • Instructional coach will observe during three intervention periods and script the moves the teacher makes. |
| • Coach and teacher will meet after each meeting and determine one activity they might try during the next observation to help keep students engaged. |
| **STUDY** |
| • After reviewing the data from each observation, we realized that the students were much more engaged when cooperative structures were in place in the classroom. |
| **ACT** |
| • The intervention teacher decided to partner with another teacher in the district to think more about using cooperative structures in their classrooms and what that might look like. |
| • The instructional coach and teacher were going to meet monthly to touch base and see what was working. |

The PDSA framework allows you to consider the plan of action in a clear, coherent, and action-focused manner. In many ways, the PDSA framework mirrors the inquiry stance discussed in Chapter 4. This framework can be used for coaching cycles (as illustrated in the previous example) or in much larger planning contexts. A tool to support your work using the PDSA cycle can be found in Appendix 15.

Once you feel confident that the larger plan has been addressed, we offer a list of ten questions that will be useful to help you think about your work as a lead learner when planning for any work you might support with learning teams. Each of the questions is linked to the research-based characteristic discussed earlier in the book. Keep in mind that it is through the connections and interactions that powerful learning takes place.

## QUESTIONS TO ASK WHILE PLANNING

| QUESTIONS | CONNECTIONS AND CONSIDERATIONS |
|---|---|
| 1. What are the goals for this learning session? Are there goals related to the larger goals of the district's learning plan? Are my goals the same as the goals of the group? How can we set the stage for learning by all sharing our hopes and intentions for the session? | These questions help us consider alignment and duration in our work. |
| 2. What do I want this group to think and feel by the end of our time together? | Content focus as well as a focus on social and emotional needs supports the end goals. |
| 3. What might their disposition be? What do I know about their emotional state? Do I anticipate the teachers will need to release emotions? If so, how can we do this productively? | Understanding the interpersonal nature of our colleagues help us consider the active learning experiences we might suggest or use. |
| 4. What do I anticipate might be challenging for them? How can I prepare for this and support them with these challenges? | Support others by being prepared and flexible. |
| 5. How can I involve them in this conversation? How can I make it matter to them? | Ownership is crucial to motivation. |

*(Continued)*

(Continued)

| QUESTIONS | CONNECTIONS AND CONSIDERATIONS |
|---|---|
| 6. Are there any materials (articles or tools) that I might gather and bring with me to support either their knowledge or emotions? | Conceptual inputs play a large role in the depth of the learning. The focus and learning of any professional learning experience must be based on solid theoretical foundations. |
| 7. What team-builder exercise will I use to start the conversation? | Begin the conversation immediately in order to create a trusting environment. |
| 8. What will the flow and the timing of the session look like? How will each session build on the next, or how does this session fit with the larger learning goals? | Think through time beforehand. |
| 9. How will we get to next steps? When during the session do we need to move toward determining next steps? | Never leave without next steps. |
| 10. How do I want to feel at the end of this learning opportunity? | As the lead learner, consider how you will know your goals have been met or how your own learning has been supported through the experience. |

*You will want to listen not only for what your participants know but also for who they are as human beings.*

This tool is available for your use in Appendix 16. Thinking about these questions beforehand and always keeping in mind the importance of listening fully to the learners you are responsible for (in one way or another) is imperative to the success of the learning.

Just as importantly, be aware of the effect of your words on the learning of the participants by being intentional about presenting ways to craft and deliver open-ended questions that probe thinking.

Hopefully we have offered much for you to think about in terms of your role as a lead learner in the professional learning situation. Our stance as the lead learner is critical—we must respond to the needs of the individuals as well as the needs of the whole group. Throughout the learning experience, we have to strive to communicate the goals and intentions effectively. And, all the while, we must work to develop trust and rapport with participants. Let's see this in action with a vignette Marisa shares about working with a group of principals in a district:

I was recently facilitating a session with a group of principals around providing powerful feedback to teachers as a part of their teacher observation model. The district had been working with their teachers for several years on shifting from a more traditional, teacher-directed way of instruction to a facilitative stance. Significant work had been done in helping teachers understand a different stance and how that impacted student learning.

While working with this group of principals, it became apparent that while they were encouraging a new stance in their teachers, they themselves did not embody that same stance when they were in the role of supporting the teachers' professional learning. Through careful questioning and discussion, the principals realized that their language and stance communicated to their teachers the very didactic model they were asking their teachers to move away from. In our work together, we spent time analyzing the questioning and feedback techniques the teachers were learning and using with their students and applying them to the feedback and discussion cycles the principals were having with their teachers.

This experience illuminated for me, as the facilitator of this learning, just how important it is to listen carefully to the experiences of the learners in the room and connect for them the work that they are doing across initiatives. Because I was familiar with their goals for their teachers, I was able to align the work and push these principals to the very learning that would make the biggest impact on their practice as educators.

## Questions for Reflection

- What does it mean for you to be the lead learner in a room of teachers?

- What is the most effective stance to take when facilitating new learning? Why? What might you need to work on when you become the lead learner?

- How will you effectively plan for your teachers' implementation of new learning? How will you consider the bigger professional learning system that you are building in your district?

# CHAPTER 6

# Connecting the Learning

Throughout this book, we have offered a broad overview of learning in our profession, discussed the value of the content that grounds our learning, explored important elements within our learning structures as well as the structures themselves, and finally the power of the role of the facilitator. In this chapter, we will make sense of how all of these attributes play out together in schools and systems. All of the attributes listed are interconnected and interdependent. For instance, we can attempt to teach teachers the content of effective phonics instruction, but without an effective facilitator who models lessons and offers participants the chance to practice, the rich content will not help shift practice. Or, we can host a fantastic day addressing equity in children's literature during back to school week with an engaging facilitator, but if we never discuss equity again, explore it in our classrooms, or offer teachers resources to use with students, teaching and learning will continue on as they always did.

> The star teachers of the twenty-first century will be those who work collaboratively to infuse the best ideas into standard practice. They will be the teachers who work every day to improve teaching—not only their own, but that of the whole profession.
>
> —Stigler, 1999

Alternatively, leading professional learning effectively does not simply involve checking boxes to make sure all attributes are addressed—it requires thoughtful conversations with all stakeholders and planning with the end goal in mind. When professional learning is successful and teachers have begun to shift their practice, it is because thoughtful and intentional decisions were made, connections with learning and across settings were seamless and recursive, and collaboration was constant. Chapter 6 makes the case for the ways in which the characteristics, mechanisms, and facilitation all come together and interact. To begin thinking about this interaction, consider Pam's story as she helps to prepare her elementary principals to lead their classroom teachers.

As educators, we try hard to make Ignacio Estrada's quote ("If a child can't learn the way we teach, maybe we should teach the way they learn") true for children in schools—do we do the same for adults and their professional learning? These words were on Pam's mind as she went to lead a group of elementary principals and literacy coaches as they crafted a math professional learning plan for the following school year.

Pam began the morning by asking the participants to think about the following questions as they reflected on their work last year:

- What successes have you and your teachers experienced?

- What was challenging?

- What are your thoughts for next year?

- What questions do you still have?

They shared many building level successes and then went on to discuss their challenges. Time was an issue—how do we fit in all the aspects of effective math instruction? They discussed schedules and how they might help. They worried about addressing the new state standards. Several shared their struggles in buildings with students who needed a tremendous amount of both academic and emotional support.

Pam then asked them to think about a powerful professional learning experience they had: "Think of a powerful professional learning experience that impacted your work. What about the staff development made it so powerful and successful?" They described collaboration, learning over time, intensity, ownership, job-embedded—all of the things known to be true about effective professional learning. She then used those two activities to guide their planning of their professional learning for next year. She began by asking these questions: "What aspect of math instruction do your teachers need to learn more about? What would be the most effective way to accomplish that learning?" Then, she organized them into groups to discuss the two questions.

The principals had thoughtful conversations in their small groups—really digging deep into their individual building's needs and the kinds of activities they could provide for their teachers to engage in throughout the school year to help their learning and growth. Once they had a list of possible professional learning activities, they began crafting action plans for their buildings that described who was responsible for what and when would it happen.

Many principals discussed the importance of their role as a lead learner in their buildings and how they might authentically engage in inquiry themselves. Some made concrete plans for their novice teachers and how they might work with their instructional coaches to get the school year off to a good start. Others crafted focus questions for their professional learning communities (PLCs) and made commitments to attend the weekly conversations. One principal mapped out weekly faculty meetings to include workshops that addressed problem solving as well as a study on a professional book that addresses this topic. Finally, another decided to learn more about the lesson study process so that her staff could explore the new state standards and their math work. Then, each principal shared their plans with one another and went through one more revision after hearing their colleagues' ideas and suggestions.

Pam offered her team of principals the chance to reflect on their teachers' individual needs and the space to make a thoughtful professional learning plan for the duration of the school year. Of course there are some aspects of this work that aren't evident—how much choice do the teachers have in their learning? Was there any follow-through with the plan? Pam has many next steps on this professional learning journey, however, she is on the right path and has already provided her principals with an opportunity to plan for some thoughtful learning for their teachers. What might the rest of the path look like, and how might the professional learning eventually impact the students in Pam's district? Let's take a moment to consider the connection and implications for student achievement.

## LEARNING DESIGN CONSIDERATIONS

While many features of effective professional learning are supported by empirical studies, some questions remain unanswered about the importance of individual components and how they might interact to impact student achievement. Clearly, professional learning that promotes a strong content focus impacts teacher learning and student achievement. However, many questions still remain. For instance, might professional learning be more effective when the content focus is paired with active learning? Or, does duration matter when content focus or active learning does not characterize the professional learning experience? Or even, how do we consider the weight and importance of each characteristic?

*Designing a research-based framework for planning and executing professional learning may increase teacher knowledge, improve teacher practice, and support growth in student achievement.*

In addition to identifying the essential characteristics of effective professional learning, a framework can highlight how essential characteristics are related to one another. It is not enough to simply check off a list of essential characteristics of effective professional learning. Professional learning providers must also consider how the essential characteristics are interdependent while also making room for additional features that may play an important role in teacher learning and student achievement.

Desimone (2009) proposes a conceptual framework (Figure 6.1) that reflects her understanding of the relationships between the essential characteristics she identified in her review of the research and the impact on teacher knowledge and student achievement. While her framework has many components of powerful professional learning, there is little to designate how they relate to each other. When we consider other important features of professional learning, the framework could change a bit.

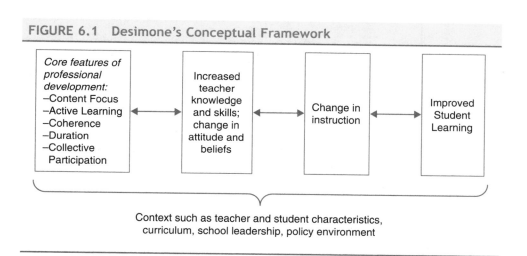

FIGURE 6.1   Desimone's Conceptual Framework

Now, let's consider the additional features of conceptual inputs and the role of the facilitator. These components also have a relationship to the content focus and active learning strategies. Therefore, a more comprehensive term could be used, like "learning design." The learning design encompasses the content focus, based on solid conceptual inputs and active learning events, and is supported by appropriate considerations for collective participation and collaboration. Additionally, in an effective learning design, the facilitator is knowledgeable and has designed the learning events based on current research in best practices and theories of learning. Rather than singularly focusing on each of those components directly, the interconnectedness of content focus and active learning with the support structures of collective participation, conceptual inputs, and the facilitator could be combined in the learning design (See Figure 6.2).

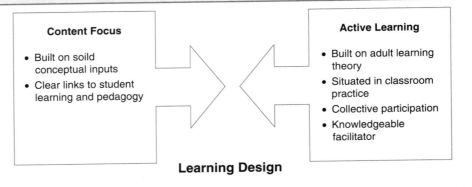

**FIGURE 6.2** Learning Design

**Content Focus**

- Built on soild conceptual inputs
- Clear links to student learning and pedagogy

**Active Learning**

- Built on adult learning theory
- Situated in classroom practice
- Collective participation
- Knowledgeable facilitator

**Learning Design**

To this end, the learning design becomes a singular characteristic of effective professional learning that is made up of research-based features. A framework begins to emerge when duration and alignment are placed in a relationship with learning design (See Figure 6.3).

With this framework in place, duration is also considered after the learning has been designed and is based on the learning goals of the designer, rather than arbitrary length of time. Coherence, both in teacher prior knowledge and state/district goals, is considered before planning the entire experience. All arrows indicate a two-way process, so that each segment of the process is continually reflected upon and redesigned, if necessary. Of course, not only do we need to understand the theoretical learning design, we must also attend to the emotional needs of our individual learners.

## CHANGE IS HARD

It is essential that designers of professional learning understand the necessity of the features and mechanisms described in this book and use this knowledge to design professional learning opportunities that build on them. In addition to understanding the features and processes, it is essential that designers of professional learning understand how to best plan for their adult learners and how changes in teachers' practice depends on change at a school level as well. However carefully designed those learning experiences are, they are just the beginning of the change process. Fullan (1992) offers a simple model for a complex process, which he named the Tier-Tier Change Process. He describes the change in three stages: Stage 1: Initiate the Change, Stage 2: Implement the Change, and Stage 3: Institutionalize the Change. You can find a tool to support your thinking around this change process in Appendix 17.

FIGURE 6.3 New Conceptual Framework for Professional Learning

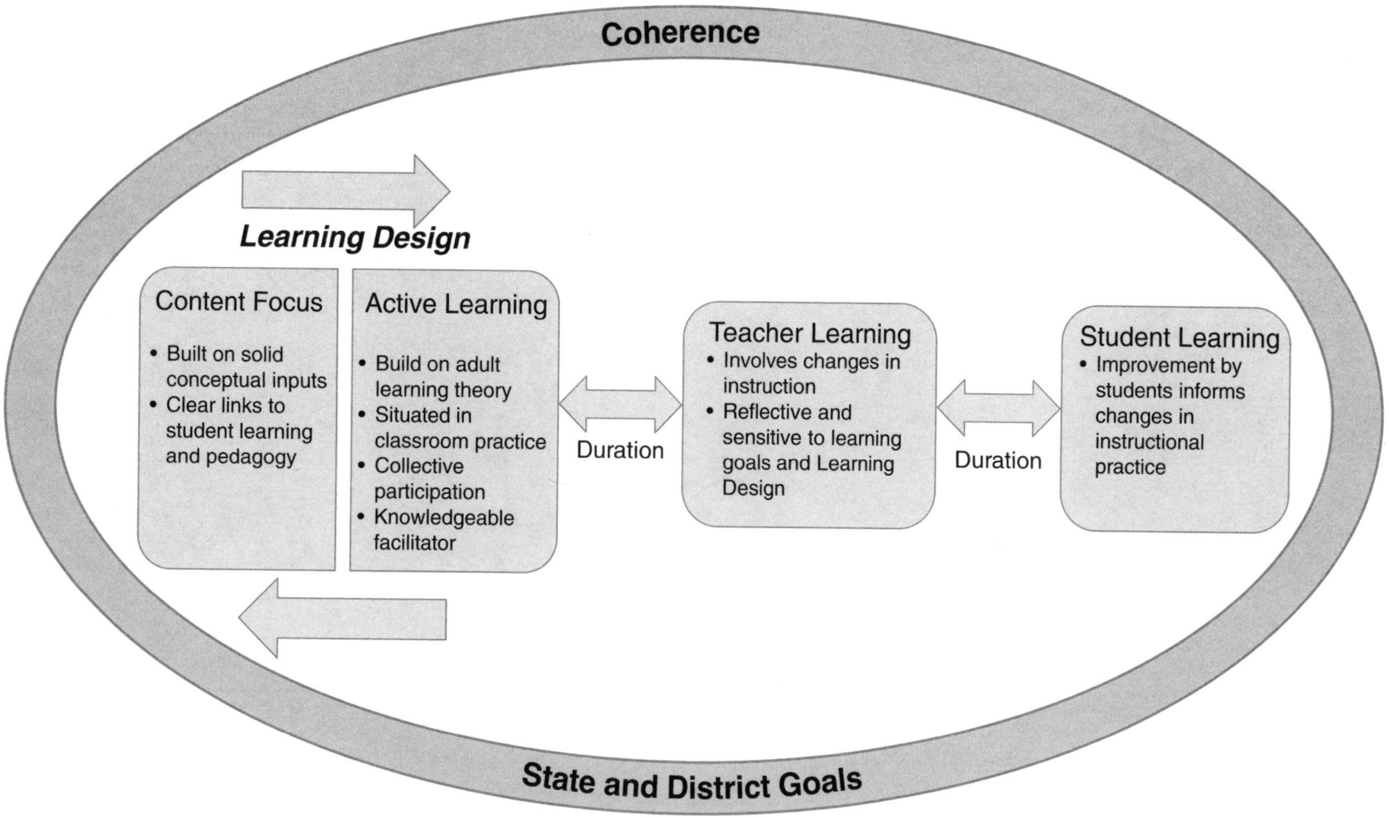

**Coherence**

*Learning Design*

**Content Focus**
- Built on solid conceptual inputs
- Clear links to student learning and pedagogy

**Active Learning**
- Build on adult learning theory
- Situated in classroom practice
- Collective participation
- Knowledgeable facilitator

Duration

**Teacher Learning**
- Involves changes in instruction
- Reflective and sensitive to learning goals and Learning Design

Duration

**Student Learning**
- Improvement by students informs changes in instructional practice

**State and District Goals**

Initiating the change in Stage 1 is a place to begin gathering input from all stakeholders. Typically, this stage is where professional learning opportunities such as speakers, workshops, institutes, and classes occur. They set the stage for the change to occur. They provide impetus, background knowledge, and connections to stakeholders and attempt to energize and excite them regarding the change. Unfortunately, this is where many changes or innovations stop. Assuming that simply increasing the knowledge of teachers or stakeholders will lead to actual change in the classroom is naïve at best. In order for true change to take place, we must focus on "increasing the capacity of the organization by placing issues of teaching and learning at the center of the dialogue among the entire school community" (Newman & Associates, 1996, p. 291).

In order for the entire school community to become involved in the change, one must move from Stage 1 in the change process to Stage 2 where the innovation is implemented. This implementation phase is where true professional learning takes place. PLCs, teacher inquiry, and instructional coaching are all powerful vehicles for beginning the work of implementing change. Those vehicles allow for the innovation to take place with integrity and provide the support necessary to sustain the change through the learning process (Fogarty & Pete, 2007).

The final stage in Fullan's model is Stage 3, institutionalizing the change. Institutionalizing a change indicates that it is now the essence of the institution's mission—it is part of the very fabric and way of work of a particular organization. Institutionalization is a long and arduous process. It requires persistence and patience and is characterized by rehearsal and repetition, obstacles and triumphs, and readiness and rewards. Achievements must be celebrated publicly so that all who are a part of the change can be recognized and the work can be acknowledged (Fogarty & Pete, 2007).

Guskey (2000) discusses the changes that one *expects* to occur rather than the process that *does* occur. Since the first tier, in essence, introduces the change, and the second tier implements the change, it is expected that teachers change their behavior when strong evidence has been put forth regarding the innovation's research history or anecdotal evidence that has been provided to show the innovation "works." Teachers, however, want to know it works with "their kids" before being willing to change. Guskey's research indicates that teachers will only think or believe differently when they see for themselves how their change in behavior led to a difference in student achievement. Consider Kelly's experience coaching Don through his plan of improvement.

Kelly, an elementary instructional coach, had been working with Don, a third-grade teacher, for almost a full year. He had been on a plan of improvement due to his inability to form relationships with his students and their subsequent poor performance on their Grade 3 state assessments. Kelly had tried many different approaches, yet Don continued to push her away and act defensive about his instructional practices. Finally, the central office purchased a new literacy program that included thoughtful instruction on comprehension, writing, and independent reading. It was research based and provided a lot of support for teachers as well as a strong social and emotional component for students. Luckily, Don's school was an early adopter, and he was expected to use the resource.

Kelly spent time in August helping Don and the rest of the third-grade team get ready to use the new resource. She also scheduled a monthly coaching session with Don to address the new curriculum. In addition, Kelly and Don's principal, Mark, coordinated a series of observations beginning in November and ending in April to not only offer Don feedback but to also begin collecting data on his performance. Kelly noticed early on in her coaching sessions that Don's stance had shifted—he was less defensive about his classroom practice and more open to her suggestions. He also seemed to feel well-supported with the new curriculum's lessons.

In March, Kelly and Mark had the chance to observe during writing time in Don's classroom. There was a busy hum of children writing and sharing their thinking. When they looked around the room, all the students were engaged—writing their fiction stories in their journals. When Kelly asked a little girl in the corner how things were going, she looked up with a smile on her face and shared that she was writing a nine-chapter story about a girl and her dog and their adventures. Kelly and Mark left and discussed the change they were seeing not only in Don but in his students.

In April, the third-grade classes all took the state assessment. Don commented to students that he thought his kids had done really well this year and attributed their success to the new resource he had begun using—as well as his one-on-one coaching time with Kelly. Come June, the state test results came back, and Don's prediction was accurate. His kids had done well, and all but one had passed—a big difference from the year before. Don no longer needed a plan of improvement, and he became a much more engaged and committed part of Mark's faculty.

As this vignette indicates, teachers who are involved in professional learning that builds on active learning strategies, collective participation over time, and is aligned with their beliefs and their context, can make changes in their instruction. In this instance, Don also needed to see the change in his students' achievement to affirm the changes he had made in his instructional practice. The professional learning plan that Kelly helped to design for Don took into account the research-based features and mechanisms, adult learning theory, and the change process. Following Kelly's lead, district-level professional learning staff should consider building long-term learning opportunities that support the kind of learning the research has shown to make the most impact on teachers and students.

This overview of school change is brief, and while the model is simple, the notions are complex. It is important to acknowledge significant issues that may arise in the implementation of the three stages. Many innovations may stall in Stage 1. Spending too much time conceptualizing, discussing, debating, and organizing may lead stakeholders to become overwhelmed. Staying in Stage 1 without moving quickly to Stage 2 may lead to perpetuation of typical notions of professional development, where teachers are told what, how, and why they must adopt a new innovation, instead of professional learning, where teachers are in control of their learning and build on what they know. Finally, without moving to Stage 3, innovations may never become part of the fabric of the instructional practices of teachers or the way that things are done at that particular institution for those particular students. It is easy to think that because teachers are using the terms and basic principles of the innovation, then it is a part of their teaching, but simply integrating catch phrases into the vocabulary of the school, doesn't mean the underlying conceptualizations of these ideas and innovations are fully understood (Fullan, 2005).

## EVALUATION—HOW DO WE KNOW IT'S WORKING?

Stakeholders are becoming increasingly interested in whether or not the cost-benefit for professional learning is leading to its intended outcomes. Unfortunately, evaluation is not often a part of the professional learning cycle beyond simple measures of participant comfort and satisfaction (King, 2013; Shaha, Lewis, O'Donnell, & Brown, 2004). If any evaluation has taken place, it is most often of an event related to professional learning and not the ongoing, job-embedded professional learning that is most effective for teacher change (Guskey, 2002).

*In order for professional learning to be the catalyst for change that it is intended to be, it must stand up to rigorous evaluation to determine if results from the learning are impacting student achievement.*

Researchers have begun to look at models of evaluating professional learning so that clear links to student achievement and teacher change are evident (Guskey, 2002; Joyce &

PROFESSIONAL LEARNING REDEFINED

Showers, 2002; Learning Forward, 2014; Shaha et al., 2004). Joellen Killion (2002) reminds us,

> We must become evaluators of our work—asking ourselves questions to elicit data so we can know what is and is not producing the impact we hope to produce.… We must be ruthless in asking for evidence and scrutinizing our own practices. To improve, we must get comfortable with the idea of routinely and critically examining our data to know if our work is producing the results we desire. (p.12)

In order to "critically examine our data," Guskey (2002) puts forth a model that evaluates professional learning on five levels that build on one another. Success at one level is necessary for success at the higher levels. Each of the five levels is described below.

## LEVEL 1: PARTICIPANTS' REACTIONS

The first level of evaluation looks at the participants' reactions and feelings about the learning. This is most similar to the "traditional" evaluations at the end of a professional development experience where participants are asked to rate the trainer, the materials, and the facilities. While to some, this type of evaluation may seem trivial and unimportant, Guskey argues that it is essential to attend to these basic human needs and that this information helps to improve the design and delivery of the learning experiences.

## LEVEL 2: PARTICIPANTS' LEARNING

The second level of evaluation measures the knowledge and skills participants gained from the learning experience. While this level of evaluation could be interpreted as a simple paper-pencil exam at the end of a workshop, more comprehensive assessments could include portfolios of artifacts, oral reflections, simulations, or demonstrations. Information gathered from this level of evaluation is used to improve the content, format, and organization of the learning. Because the measures used in this level must indicate the level of proficiency, the indicators of successful learning must be determined prior to the learning taking place.

## LEVEL 3: ORGANIZATIONAL SUPPORT AND CHANGE

Level 3 shifts the attention from the practitioner to the organization. As we described earlier, alignment within the organization is critical to the successful implementation of the learning. If the organization, which could include the school, district, or state, does not have the infrastructure to support the change, then it essentially negates the progress made at Levels 1 and 2 (Sparks & Hirsh, 1997). Evaluation at this level is more complex and requires careful alignment to the professional learning. The data collected not only help make decisions about future change initiatives but also inform stakeholders of the support and resources needed.

## LEVEL 4: PARTICIPANTS' USE OF NEW KNOWLEDGE AND SKILLS

At Level 4, the evaluation centers on whether or not the change in knowledge and skills has transferred to the actual practice of teachers. Unlike the evaluation at Level 2, which simply assesses whether or not the participant had acquired the knowledge or skills, this level assesses the transfer of that knowledge or skill to the instructional practice of the teacher. This level of evaluation is more complex due to the fact that implementation of innovation is often a gradual and uneven process (Guskey, 2002). It is clear that professional learning that takes place in PLCs requires a significant amount of time, collaboration, and support in order for the new practices to be integrated fully into the teachers' repertoire (Killion, 2006), therefore data collection at this level is not a "one time" event; rather it would take place multiple times over a significant duration. Data collection and evaluation at this level might include structured interviews, observations, portfolios, or review of video.

## LEVEL 5: STUDENT LEARNING OUTCOMES

Level 5 addresses the "bottom line": Does the professional learning affect student achievement? This is the "primary reason" to evaluate professional learning (Joyce & Showers, 2002, p. 95). Because professional learning and student achievement in schools is such a complicated set of variables, it is not possible to "prove" whether or not the professional learning as a singular act is responsible for student achievement (Guskey & Sparks, 1996). Furthermore, it is rare that a school is involved in singular innovation; rather, schools are working on many innovations simultaneously (Fullan, 1992).

Multiple measures are especially important to collect at this level (Joyce, 1993). Even when the learning outcomes are clear, multiple measures could highlight unintended consequences of the innovation. Data collection at this level typically includes cognitive measures of student achievement and performance such as standardized tests and grades. Other measures that could be included are affective measures or measures of change within the organization (i.e., enrollment in advanced classes, participation in activities, attendance rates, or discipline referrals).

## USING AN EVALUATION MODEL

It is clear that in the current age of accountability, professional learning must be an investment that delivers on both teacher and student performance that can be verified (Guskey, 2002; Joyce & Showers, 2002; Shaha et al., 2004; Todnem & Warner, 1993). Each of the five levels described in the previous section are integral to the continuous improvement of the professional learning of teachers and students. The data collected at each level represent an important area of focus to refine and improve innovation efforts.

While evaluation is usually considered to be a culminating event, it is essential that evaluation methods be considered before the innovation begins. Beginning with the end in mind or "backward planning" is typically addressed when evaluating student learning (Wiggins & McTighe, 2005); however, it is also essential to begin the planning of the professional learning with the student achievement targets as the beginning (Earley & Porritt, 2013; Guskey, 2001). If one starts with the desired outcomes in student achievement and then works backward to identify what the instructional practices would look like, what support and resources are necessary at the organizational level, what knowledge and skills teachers would need and how they would best be learned, the professional learning planning would be efficient, and the evaluation methods would be integrated from the beginning. Combining this planning/evaluation model with the structures of a PLC that encourages inquiry leads teachers to not only plan for their own professional learning but also to take charge of it. Additionally, when the evaluation and planning of professional learning is in the hands of those who will use it most, it allows for flexibility within the professional learning. Even if student outcomes are similar, the methods for achieving the outcomes are context specific. What works with one group of students and teachers may not transfer to another context. "What works always depends on where, when and with whom" (Guskey, 2002, p. 50).

It is essential that the work of evaluating professional learning happens within the context of a PLC. PLCs provide the structure and support that allow for the evaluation process to take place in an authentic and meaningful manner. The questions that are formulated at each step in the process are part of the professional learning of the members of the PLC. Keeping in mind that teachers need to see evidence of success early in order to change their practice, evidence must be gathered within the first month of implementation (Kreider & Bouffard, 2006). When evaluation is only shared at the end of an experience, disappointment is a possibility because there was little opportunity for correction (Joyce & Showers, 2002).

## PUTTING IT ALL TOGETHER

Now that we've explored the design, change process, and evaluation, how might you begin to consider putting the essential pieces together? In this next section, we will unpack the planning necessary to move an innovation forward. We will link many of the processes and mechanisms described through the book and provide an example of a comprehensive plan. We have created a planning and guidance document for your use (see Appendix 17). After each narrative, a small portion of the document will be shown as an illustration.

## STUDENT OUTCOMES

Let's begin as many have suggested, with the student outcomes at the center of our work. What do we want our students to know and be able to do? The answer may come from student data, teacher conversations, or observations of student work. Beginning with the end in mind helps us begin with what we want to see in our students. As an example, let's say our student outcome is that we want our students to have deeper, thoughtful conversations about text. We've noticed that in many classrooms, traditional, teacher-directed instruction still dominates language arts instruction. Student conversation is limited, and when it happens, it tends to be shallow in content. We know that for our students to truly analyze text at deep levels, they need to be able to have thoughtful conversations about their work.

---

**Student Outcome:**

What do we want our students to be able to know and do?

*We want our students to have deeper, more thoughtful conversations about text. We see this as a need from the shift in the standards and for our students to take ownership of their learning.*

---

## TEACHER OUTCOMES

From there, we can begin to formulate the teacher outcomes. If we want something different in our students, then what do we need our teachers to be able to know and do? Continuing with the example, if we want our students to have deeper, more thoughtful conversations about text, then our teachers need to know how to plan lessons that allow for student conversation, and they need to know how to facilitate student conversations that allow for student thinking to take center stage. Teachers are currently relying on more direct recall questions than "meatier" questions that allow for student thinking to emerge.

---

**Teacher Outcome:**

If we want the above, what do we need our teachers to be able to know and do?

- *Know how to plan lessons that allow for student conversation, both in time and quality of prompts*

- *Know how to facilitate student conversations that allow for student thinking to take center stage*

---

## DURATION AND EVALUATION

Now that we have our outcomes established, we can outline our duration. We know clearly that teachers (and students) need significant time to learn, try new strategies, and evaluate the outcomes. Let's consider a three-year timeline for this learning. We are asking teachers to change an instructional practice in a significant way. The first year, our focus will be on building knowledge of facilitating conversations and crafting questions that allow for students to grapple with making meaning. We can see conceptual inputs taking a big role in this part of the learning. The second year, our focus will be on practicing writing questions and allowing time for student conversations with feedback from each other. Year 3 will look similar to Year 2 with refined feedback. Evaluating progress at the end of each year will allow for refinement and readjustment.

---

**Time Frame:**

### Year 1

○ *Build knowledge*

- Common readings on student talk in classrooms

- Common readings on facilitating conversations

- Analysis of curricular materials for support in student conversations

---

*(Continued)*

(Continued)

| |
|---|
| ○ *Evaluation* <br>     ▪ Initial attempts <br>     ▪ Content knowledge <br>     ▪ Teacher feedback |
| **Year 2** <br> ○ *Practice/Feedback* <br>     ▪ Initial attempts with support <br>     ▪ Feedback from coaches/administrators <br> ○ *Evaluation* <br>     ▪ Observations <br>     ▪ Teacher feedback |
| **Year 3** <br> ○ *Refinement* <br>     ▪ Continued practice in classrooms <br>     ▪ Refinement of language <br> ○ *Evaluation* <br>     ▪ Observations: time spent in teacher-directed instruction vs. student led instruction <br>     ▪ Teacher feedback |

## CONTENT FOCUS

From the timeline, we can begin to consider the way this learning is situated in the content area. It's also important to consider the curricular materials teachers have at their disposal. Do the materials have support for this kind of instruction, or may they hinder the work? For our example, we will consider elementary teachers and will situate this learning in the language arts block. Their current curricular materials for language arts do not have support for this kind of instruction. We will need to consider how to supplement their current materials.

---

**Content Focus:**

How does this professional learning fit within content? How do the current curricular materials support or hinder this learning?

- Within the 120 minute literacy block, elementary teachers have multiple opportunities to support student conversation.

- Shared reading, interactive read alouds, mentor text analysis, and peer review of writing are a few opportunities to support this initiative.

- Current curricular materials have little support for teachers in this aspect of literacy development.

  - *Current materials allow for mostly teacher-to-student and student-to-teacher dialogue only. Student-to-student dialogue is rarely introduced.*

  - *Teachers will need significant support in reframing some of the dialogue into student-student interactions.*

  - *Teachers will need support in refining some of the questions within the curriculum to support a conversation rather than an answer.*

  - *Consider this aspect of the work heavily when adopting new curriculum (in two years).*

---

## COHERENCE

Our next step is to consider the coherence of this innovation alongside the others in the district or school. A series of questions might help us establish how coherent this learning will be alongside other factors.

- What other initiatives/focus might schools have? How will this fit with that work?

- How will this innovation be communicated to all stakeholders?

- What mechanisms exist currently for professional learning? How will they be used for this work?

- What other groups may be impacted by this work (e.g., Title 1, special education, administrators)? How will they be a part of the learning?

- What infrastructure mechanisms might need to be addressed (instructional time, grading practices) that would impact or hinder this learning?

When we consider the above questions, we begin to think about the context within which the learning will take place. By considering the context, we can make plans for and often circumvent some of the issues that commonly hinder the learning from taking place or taking root.

---

**Coherence:**

- **Current initiatives**

  ○ Teacher observation model—clear support within the new model for student conversations. Support teachers in understanding the links.

  ○ STEAM—depth of student conversations will help deepen understandings in all subject areas. In Year 3 of our innovation, we will consider whether or not we see transfer of a facilitative stance and student-led conversations in other parts of day.

- **Mechanisms for professional learning**

  ○ Initial learning—two scheduled inservice days will be devoted to sessions that support initial learning

  ○ Dedicated time for PLC meetings—reconsider how much time is spent for this initiative versus teacher choice in PLCs

- **Infrastructure**

  ○ Grading practice will need to be addressed—if we are asking teachers to devote more time to student conversations, then time for other types of instruction (i.e., worksheets) is reduced. How will they get grades?

---

## LEARNING DESIGN

We are now ready to address the learning design. How will our teachers interact with the learning we have set forward. This aspect of the planning needs to be fluid. We may begin our planning with just the first year outline or sketch out all three years. This is the place to keep in mind the framework discussed earlier in the chapter. How will the design include conceptual inputs? Who will facilitate the work, and why? What learning should be done as a large group, and what should be done in grade-level or other small groups? Our example continues below with an outline of the learning for Year 1.

The example that we share here is just that, an example. There are many ways that learning can unfold. The most important thing that we can keep in mind is that we consider all that we know from the research on professional learning and situate it within the context that we have in front of us. It is truly the complex ecosystem in which we do our work that is the biggest consideration for our planning. You can find the comprehensive planning document used above (Planning for Sustained Professional Learning) in Appendix 18.

---

**Learning Design:**

Considering the previous example, how will teachers interact with the learning? Using the columns below, consider how the learning can be situated in the three columns. What protocols might support the learning? What conceptual inputs will help? Where might a workshop make sense? Who will facilitate this learning?

**Year 1**

- *Teachers will attend an interactive workshop by an outside facilitator on the importance of conversation as an instructional technique. The workshop will be facilitated in a way that allows for the teachers to engage in conversation as their main form of learning.*

- *Inquiry will be kicked off on the same day. Teachers will be encouraged to frame a "wondering" around the amount or quality of student talk in their classrooms. Teachers will have significant choice in how this unfolds.*

*(Continued)*

---

(Continued)

| PLC | Coaches | Inquiry |
|---|---|---|
| How will PLCs be structured to support this work? How will teachers have voice and choice? How might they direct their own learning? | • What is the role of the coach? How will they be supported in their own learning? What expectations do they have for supporting ongoing learning? | • How might inquiry be framed around this innovation? How will inquiry dovetail with the PLC work? |
| • First semester PLC meetings will be dedicated to common readings, curricular analysis, and first attempts at drafting conversation prompts. Student evidence and work will be shared in PLC meetings throughout the second semester to support learning and refinement. | • Support the initial learning by participating in a follow-up workshop from the same facilitator that lead the whole group learning.<br><br>• Focus on learning alongside teachers in PLC meetings.<br><br>• Attend monthly coach meetings as a PLC member to share learning across schools. | • Teachers and coaches will consider a "wondering" related to the initial step of teacher talk vs. student talk in their schools and classrooms.<br><br>• The inquiry will be woven into the PLC meetings structure by supporting teachers in considering what they're learning and how that is actualized in the classroom as initial attempts. |

## CONCLUSION

We know that to "develop" teachers is not enough to have the sustained, lasting change we need in education. Teachers must have the skills to change and respond on a daily (if not more) basis. They must be learners. Powerful professional learning is the key for the change our schools and our students need. Teachers who are empowered to inquire into their own practice and seek out new information can transform the learning of the their students. Inquiry coupled with effective coaching and mentoring can lead to powerful professional learning in the classrooms and learning environments and with the students that the change is meant to impact. When inquiry, coaching, and powerful professional learning are combined under the umbrella of a PLC, teachers and all educational professionals can be engaged in the collaborative, cohesive, and content-rich learning that our students deserve. Let's re-invision Kimrey's experience as a novice teacher from Chapter 1.

As a young teacher, Kimrey felt well-supported by both her school district and the staff in the building in which she was teaching. Kimrey's first-grade classroom was right next to her mentor teacher's room, Paula. Paula made sure to connect daily with Kimrey and always had an open-door policy. Luckily, Kimrey had a very capable teaching assistant so she was able to leave her students in good hands and observe in Paula's room often. Paula and Kimrey planned lessons together, and Kimrey had the chance to see the instructional techniques they discussed play out in Paula's capable hands before trying them herself.

Every morning when Kimrey entered Paula's classroom, she was struck by a poster that was on the wall of Paula's room—it affirmed her teaching practice and made her determined to continue to learn and grow. It was a black and white picture of Haim Ginott with the following quote printed on it: "I've come to a frightening conclusion that I am the decisive element in the classroom. It's my personal approach that creates the climate. It's my daily mood that makes the weather. As a teacher, I possess a tremendous power to make a child's life miserable or joyous. I can be a tool of torture or an instrument of inspiration. I can humiliate or heal. In all situations, it is my response that decides whether a crisis will be escalated or de-escalated and a child humanized or dehumanized." Kimrey felt the importance of this quote to her core and knew that in her classroom, her students felt joyful, and she was able to help heal her youngsters who were in crisis. Her routines were clear and consistent, and her students seemed to feel safe. Kimrey was beginning to plan more effectively for her guided reading lesson, and her students were learning to read!

Kimrey was also lucky to have a strong first-grade PLC. Of course, Paula was a part of this group, but there were also three other teachers who supported Kimrey in her growth as a novice teacher. One of these teachers was new to the field also, and she served as a learner alongside Kimrey—they often shopped together for their classrooms and asked one another silly questions that they were embarrassed to ask their more experienced teammates.

Kimrey attended her district's professional learning sessions for primary new teachers that were designed to help them learn more about effective early literacy practices and always left with a deeper understanding of how a child learns to read as well as something new to try in her classroom. She participated in her state's novice teacher assistance program and taught a small group phonics lesson in her district's core literacy program for her struggling readers during her observation so that she might get some helpful feedback about what was working and what she might need to tweak.

At the end of her first year, Kimrey was so excited to spend the summer participating in a Writing Across the Curriculum course her local university was offering. She knew she had done a great job working with her students in their morning writing journals, but she really wanted to make writing a richer experience for her students during the next school year. Her principal was thrilled to have her return in the fall as he was impressed with her engagement and commitment. The parents of her students raved about her enthusiasm and how happy their children were in her classroom. One parent even wrote in an e-mail about his son, "Emerson has thrived this year in first grade! He loves school, and most importantly, he loves to read! He feels really confident about his ability to tackle text that might be challenging. Kimrey is absolutely a star teacher, and I sure hope Emerson has the opportunity to have lots more like her over the course of his school career."

## Questions for Reflection

- How do the features and mechanisms of effective professional learning in the previous chapters mutually support and interact with one another in the setting in which you work?

- What might you want to consider now when evaluating professional learning in your district? What is your new learning?

# Appendix 1

## Curricular Resource Planning Tool

Use this tool to support your thinking about how to use curricular resources in planning for professional learning. Consider the coherence between the materials teachers have and the desired instructional strategies.

| INSTRUCTIONAL STRATEGY | DOES THE CURRICULUM ADDRESS THIS STRATEGY? IF NOT, HOW WILL IT BE ADDED? | HOW THE CURRICULUM ADDRESSES THE STRATEGY | POSSIBLE MISCONCEPTIONS/ AREAS OF GROWTH | PROFESSIONAL LEARNING EXPERIENCES | ONGOING LEARNING |
|---|---|---|---|---|---|
|  |  |  |  |  |  |
|  |  |  |  |  |  |
|  |  |  |  |  |  |
|  |  |  |  |  |  |
|  |  |  |  |  |  |
|  |  |  |  |  |  |

Available for download at **resources.corwin.com/RedefiningProfessionalLearning**

# Appendix 2

## Planning for a Brief Professional Learning Session

- **SET THE STAGE:** Ask, *What do you want to know about the topic we are discussing?* In order to explore this question fully, you might use one of the following protocols:

  - Create a KWL chart (Know, Want to Know, Learn)
  - Brainstorm and discuss the challenges inherent in the topic
  - Visualize ways we want our schools to be

- **WHY:** Share what the research tells us about the topic—offer conceptual inputs to support the participants learning:

  - Read article on the topic, and discuss the reading using a text rendering protocol
  - Watch a video or explore a graphic

- **HOW:** Show how it is accomplished in classrooms:

  - Lesson experience through model or video
  - Offer opportunities for teachers to participate as readers and writers
  - Read lesson plans
  - Explore student work

- **DEBRIEF:** Reflect in order to make the learning our own:

  - Next steps, practice
  - Connect, reconnect, collect

Planning for a Brief Professional Learning Session

# TOPIC:

| |
|---|
| 1. Determine what the participants already know and then want to learn about the topic. "What do you know about _____? Now, what do you want to know about _____?" |
| 2. Share the current research and best practices on _____. |
| 3. Offer an example of _____ in action—a videotaped example, a model lesson, a lesson plan, or so on. |
| 4. Debrief the experience. Ask, "What did you notice?" |

# Appendix 3

## Reflecting on Effective Elements of Professional Learning

| ELEMENT | HOW IS THIS ELEMENT ADDRESSED IN THIS LEARNING EXPERIENCE(S)? | HOW IS THIS ELEMENT INTERACTING WITH THE OTHER ELEMENTS TO SUPPORT STRONG PROFESSIONAL LEARNING? |
|---|---|---|
| **Active Learning**<br>• Are teachers directly engaged in constructing knowledge (discussions, observations, etc.)?<br>• Are they applying newly learned skills?<br>• Are the activities they engage in similar to the ones we might offer to students in classrooms? | | How does active learning interact with . . .<br>Coherence?<br>Collaboration?<br>Duration? |
| **Coherence**<br>• Are the goals of the professional learning aligned or congruent with district and school goals? | | How does coherence interact with . . .<br>Active learning?<br>Collaboration?<br>Duration? |
| **Collaboration**<br>• Partnerships?<br>• Grade-level teams?<br>• Schoolwide endeavors? | | How does collaboration interact with . . .<br>Active learning?<br>Coherence?<br>Duration? |
| **Duration**<br>• Is the professional learning ongoing? | | How does duration interact with . . .<br>Active learning?<br>Coherence?<br>Collaboration? |

Available for download at **resources.corwin.com/RedefiningProfessionalLearning**

# Appendix 4

## Four Corners (20–30 minutes)

Adapted from Center for the Collaborative Classroom's *Caring School Communities* (2018)

| STEP | FACILITATION TIP | NOTES |
|---|---|---|
| Prework: Place signs in the four corners of the room that read:<br>1. Agree<br>2. Strongly Agree<br>3. Disagree<br>4. Strongly Disagree | | |
| 1. Explain that you will make a statement and give participants time to think. When you say, "GO," participants will move to the corner of the room that accurately reflects how they feel about the statement and then have a conversation with the participants in their corner. | | |
| 2. Make some simple statements such as:<br>• I like to do things outdoors<br>• I like to create things<br>• I like to try new foods<br>• I like to play sports | Wait for participants to go to their corner. Allow time for all to share. | |
| 3. Ask, what did you learn about your colleagues? | | |

Available for download at **resources.corwin.com/RedefiningProfessionalLearning**

# Appendix 5

## Compass Points (20–30 minutes)

Adapted from the National School Reform Faculty

| STEP | FACILITATION TIP | NOTES |
|---|---|---|
| Prework: Place four signs on each wall in the room—North, South, East, and West. | | |
| 1. Explain the compass points:<br><br>**NORTH**: *Acts—let's do it! Let's plunge in and get things accomplished.*<br><br>**SOUTH**: *Cares—likes to know that everyone's feelings have been taken into consideration and their voices heard.*<br><br>**EAST**: *Speculates—likes to look at the big picture before acting.*<br><br>**WEST**: *Pays attention to detail—likes to know the who, what, when, where, and why.* | | |
| 2. Invite participants to reflect on their predominate direction. | Explain that no one is only one direction. | |
| 3. Ask participants to move to the direction of their choice. | | |
| 4. Once participants are grouped by compass points, ask them to discuss the following three questions:<br><br>• What are the strengths of your "direction"?<br><br>• What are the limitations of your "direction"?<br><br>• What do others need to know about you in order to work together successfully? | Give them the chance to reflect on the questions first. | |
| 5. Have a representative from each direction share the highlights of their conversation. | | |

# Appendix 6

## Setting Norms (30–40 minutes)

Adapted from The Center for the Collaborative Classroom's *Caring School Community* (2018)

| STEP | FACILITATION TIP | NOTES |
|---|---|---|
| 1. Ask participants to bring paper and pencil and gather in a circle. | Check to see that everyone can see everyone else. Pair adjacent participants. | |
| 2. Explain that one step in building a community as we begin to work together is agreeing on norms that define how we will interact with each other. | | |
| 3. Have participants close their eyes. Ask the following questions or some of your own.<br><br>Q: Think about coming to our meeting. How do you feel about being part of this group? What do you like about how we work together and treat one another? What would you like to be different?<br><br>Q: In a discussion, you want to voice an opinion that differs from the majority opinion. What would help you voice that opinion? How do you want your idea to be treated? | Pause after each question to allow them to visualize. | |

*(Continued)*

| STEP | FACILITATION TIP | NOTES |
|---|---|---|
| Q: Someone has a problem with something that you have done. How would you want them to handle this? How would you want to respond?<br><br>Q: Your teaching methods differ radically from those of a colleague with whom you are planning. How would you want to interact with that person? | | |
| 4. Have participants open their eyes and talk in pairs of two about what they thought about as they heard the questions. | | |
| 5. Ask partners to write at least two norms that reflect how they want to treat one another, using "we will" statements. | | |
| 6. As partners share their norms with the group, record them on chart paper titled "Our Norms." | Combine similar ideas as you go. | |
| 7. Use "think, pair, share" to have partners review the list and discuss whether there are any norms that they cannot agree to live by. | If necessary, modify these difficult norms so that everyone agrees. | |

Available for download at **resources.corwin.com/RedefiningProfessionalLearning**

# Appendix 7

## Chalk Talk (20–30 minutes)

Adapted from the National School Reform Faculty

| STEP | FACILITATION TIP | NOTES |
|---|---|---|
| Prework: Post a large piece of paper on the wall. Place a bucket of markers near the wall for participants to use. Alternatively, use a chalkboard and chalk. Determine a relevant question for the group. | | |
| 1. Explain to participants that this a quiet activity. No one should talk, but everyone can add to the Chalk Talk as they please. | Emphasize the importance of quiet. Sidebar conversations dilute the power of the protocol. | |
| 2. Write a relevant question or topic at the top or center of the paper or the chalkboard. | Begin handing markers/chalk to participants. | |
| 3. Allow wait time. | Sit back and watch the Chalk Talk unfold or begin circling or drawing lines to connect items. You might even jot questions or comments next to participants posts. Remember, this is a silent activity. and you will want to allow plenty of wait time before you decide that the Chalk Talk is complete. | |
| 4. When everyone is through, have participants turn to a neighbor and discuss the following question: What do you notice? | | |

# Appendix 8

## Quote Cards (20–30 minutes)

1. Create small groups of 4–5.

2. Place 4–5 quotes on the table from different authors that express different views about the topic you are discussing.

3. Have each person choose one quote and spend some time reflecting on why they chose their particular quote.

4. Allow each person to share with their small group the reason they chose their quote and what they believe is important about it.

5. When everyone has shared, have the small group members reflect on what they learned from this discussion.

Quote Cards Planning:

| Groups: |
| --- |
| |
| **Quotes to be Used:**<br>1.<br><br>2.<br><br>3.<br><br>4. |
| **Reflections/Notes:**<br><br><br> |

# Appendix 9

## Philosophical Chairs (20–30 minutes)

1. Choose and post a controversial statement for participants to either agree or disagree.

2. Set up two rows of chairs facing one another. One side for participants who agree with the statement; the other side for those who disagree.

3. Have participants move to one row or the other, depending on their belief or opinion.

4. Participants then take turns defending their position and may switch sides at any time.

5. Three rules guide the discussion:

   1. One person speaks at a time.

   2. Everyone must have a turn before someone speaks twice.

   3. You must repeat what the person on the opposing side said before you share your opinion.

6. Serve as the moderator, helping speakers to stay on topic, encouraging all to speak, and asking additional probing questions to keep the discussion going.

**Controversial Statement:**

**Set Up:**

- Chairs in rows facing each other.
- Participants may move or change their position at any time.
- Three Rules:
  - One person speaks at a time.
  - Everyone must have a turn before someone speaks twice.
  - You must repeat what the person on the opposing side said before you share your opinion.

**Reflections/Notes:**

# Appendix 10

## Consultancy Protocol (30–60 minutes)

Adapted from the School Reform Initiative

Number of Ideal Participants: 4–8

| STEP | FACILITATION TIP | NOTES FOR PLANNING |
|---|---|---|
| 1. Choose one person to be the presenter. | | |
| 2. The presenter shares a dilemma that he or she is currently struggling with. | It is important that the dilemma be phrased as a question. | |
| 3. The rest of the participants can then ask the presenter clarifying and probing questions. | | |
| 4. After responding to both the clarifying and probing questions, the presenter than restates the initial dilemma question. | It may have changed based upon the questions. | |
| 5. Then, the rest of the group has a conversation about the presenter's dilemma. | The presenter can listen and take notes but cannot participate in the discussion. | |
| 6. The presenter shares what he or she learned from listening to the conversation. | This protocol can be repeated often as part of inquiry groups or PLCs. | |

Available for download at **resources.corwin.com/RedefiningProfessionalLearning**

# Appendix 11

## Final Word (approx. 45 minutes)

Adapted from National School Reform Faculty

| STEPS | FACILITATION TIP | NOTES FOR PLANNING |
|---|---|---|
| 1. Create small groups of 4-5 participants. | | |
| 2. Provide a common text for reading (short piece). | Consider a piece that pushes on participants' thinking or is a addressing a common dilemma. | |
| 3. Set up the reading by asking participants to read the text and choose an idea or point from the text that resonates with them or has implications for their work. | Consider asking participants to choose a "back up" idea in case another participant selects the same idea. | |
| 4. Participants read and select the most salient idea. | | |
| 5. The first person to take a turn should describe (in 3 minutes or less) why their section resonated for them. | Consider asking each group to select a "time keeper." | |
| 6. The rest of the group then responds to the point discussed (up to 3 minutes). | | |
| 7. After the group discussion, the person who started the initial response has the "final word" for one minute. | | |
| 8. Continue around the group until everyone else has had a chance to share their section and the others respond. | After each group has finished, consider a whole group discussion to bring all ideas forward. | |

# Appendix 12

## Archetypal Spaces for Learning

David Thornburg identified three archetypal spaces for learning—the campfire, the watering hole, and the cave (Davis & Kappler-Hewitt, 2013).

1. The campfire is a space where people gather together to learn from an expert or in a large group.

2. The watering hole is an informal space where peers can share information and discoveries.

3. The cave is a private space where an individual can think and reflect.

   Consider your goals. What are your questions or prompts for supporting this protocol in your learning session?

| Campfire: |
| --- |
|  |

| Watering Hole: |
| --- |
|  |

| Cave: |
| --- |
|  |

# Appendix 13

## Preparing for and Debriefing a Demonstration Lesson (20–30 minutes)

| STEPS | RATIONALE |
|---|---|
| 1. Partner participants. | This allows for a safe space to share initial thinking without sharing with the whole group. |
| 2. Ask an open-ended question to frame the learning. | Example: What challenges are you facing in teaching and learning? What are some of the reasons for those challenges? What are you considering as ways to overcome said challenges? |
| 3. Consider the following questions as guidance for specific "look fors" in the demonstration lesson:<br>• What did you notice about the students' thinking or behavior?<br>• What techniques did the teacher use to support student learning?<br>• What evidence do you have that the lesson goals were met?<br>• What in the lesson allowed this to happen? | Participants should consider their challenges and think about which of these questions support evidence gathering. Specificity helps frame the lesson in supporting the individual. |
| 4. Debrief in partnerships. | Partners should have a chance to frame their challenge again and say more about what they saw in the lesson to support new thinking. |
| 5. Facilitate a whole group discussion. | This allows all participants to learn from each other. Partners may also support their learning by citing the learning and observations of their partners. |

# Facilitator Planning Sheet for Planning for and Debriefing a Demonstration Lesson

**Participants/Partnerships:**

**Questions to Frame the Observation:**

**Guidance to Support Specific Look Fors:**

- What did you notice about the students' thinking or behavior?
- What techniques did the teacher use to support student learning?
- What evidence do you have that the lesson goals were met?
- What in the lesson allowed _____ to happen?

**Others:**

**Notes from Debrief (Partners and Whole Group):**

# Appendix 14

## Planning for a Twitter Chat

| | |
|---|---|
| **Moderators:** | |
| 1. _____ | (Poses questions) |
| 2. _____ | (Pushes thinking) |

**Q1:**

(Definition of the topic)
Links? Images? Quotes?

**Q2:**

Links? Images? Quotes?

**Q3:**

Links? Images? Quotes?

**Q4:**

Links? Images? Quotes?

**Q5:**

Links? Images? Quotes?

**Q6:**

(Feel-good send off for participants)
Links? Images? Quotes?

Available for download at **resources.corwin.com/RedefiningProfessionalLearning**

# Appendix 15

## PDSA Cycle

| PLAN |
|---|
| Participants: |
| Goal: |
| Timeline: |
| Tasks: |
| |

| DO |
|---|
| |
| |

| STUDY |
|---|
| |
| |

| ACT |
|---|
| 1. |
| |
| 2. |
| |
| 3. |

# Appendix 16

## Questions to Ask While Planning

| QUESTIONS | CONNECTIONS AND CONSIDERATIONS |
|---|---|
| 1. What are the goals for this learning session? Are there goals related to the larger goals of the district's learning plan? Are my goals the same as the goals of the group? How can we set the stage for learning by all sharing our hopes and intentions for the session? | |
| 2. What do I want this group to think and feel by the end of our time together? | |
| 3. What might their disposition be? What do I know about their emotional state? Do I anticipate the teachers will need to release emotions? If so, how can we do this productively? | |
| 4. What do I anticipate might be challenging for them? How can I prepare for this and support them with these challenges? | |
| 5. How can I involve them in this conversation? How can I make it matter to them? | |
| 6. Are there any materials (articles or tools) that I might gather and bring with me to support either their knowledge or emotions? | |
| 7. What team-builder exercise will I use to start the conversation? | |
| 8. What will the flow and the timing of the session look like? How will each session build on the next, or how does this session fit with the larger learning goals? | |
| 9. How will we get to next steps? When during the session do we need to move toward determining next steps? | |
| 10. How do I want to feel at the end of this learning opportunity? | |

Available for download at **resources.corwin.com/RedefiningProfessionalLearning**

# Appendix 17

## Planning the Change Process

| STAGE | I. INITIATE THE CHANGE | II. IMPLEMENT THE CHANGE | III. INSTITUTIONALIZE THE CHANGE |
|---|---|---|---|
| **Possible Activities** | • Gather input from stakeholders<br>• Offer speakers, workshops, professional learning activities<br>• Assess participants' reaction to change to ensure buy-in—through exit surveys, or so on | • Use PLCs, instructional coaching, and inquiry to support learning<br>• Measure knowledge and skills learned from experiences<br>• Pay close attention to alignment of professional learning | • Persistence and patience is required!<br>• Celebrate successes!<br>• Assess transfer of knowledge into teacher practice—over time and through interviews, observations, portfolios, videos, and so on<br>• Begin to look at student achievement through standardized tests and grades. |
| **Action Steps** | | | |

Available for download at **resources.corwin.com/RedefiningProfessionalLearning**

# Appendix 18

## Planning for Sustained Professional Learning

**Student Outcome:**
*What do we want our students to be able to know and do?*



**Teacher Outcome:**
*If we want the above, what do we need our teachers to be able to know and do?*



**Time Frame:**

**Year One:**

**Year Two:**

**Year Three:**

*How long will we have to do this work? Consider the goals and the coherence with other initiatives. What is realistic? Consider breaking the teacher outcome into yearly goals. Include evaluation topics for each year.*



**Content Focus:**
*How does this professional learning fit within content? How do the current curricular materials support or hinder this learning*

**Coherence:**

*What other initiatives/focus might schools have? How will this fit with that work? How will this be communicated to all stakeholders? What mechanisms exist currently for professional learning? How will they be used for this work? What other groups may be impacted by this work (Title 1, special education, administrators)? How will they be a part of the learning? What infrastructure mechanisms might need to be addressed (instructional time, grading practices) that would impact or hinder this learning?*

**Learning Design:**

*Considering the above, how will teachers interact with the learning? Using the columns below, consider how the learning can be situated in the three columns. What protocols might support the learning? What conceptual inputs will help? Where might a workshop make sense? Who will facilitate this learning?*

| PLC | Coaches | Inquiry |
|---|---|---|
| *How will PLCs be structured to support this work? How will teachers have voice and choice? How might they direct their own learning?* | *What is the role of the coach? How will they be supported in their own learning? What expectations do they have for supporting ongoing learning?* | *How might inquiry be framed around this innovation? How will inquiry dovetail with the PLC work?* |

# References

Aguilar, E. (2013). *The art of coaching: Effective strategies for school transformation.* San Francisco, CA: Jossey-Bass.

Allen, J. P., Pianta, R. C., Gregory, A., Mikami, A. Y., & Lun, J. (2011). An interaction-based approach to enhancing secondary school instruction and student achievement. *Science, 333*(6045), 1034–1037.

American Federation of Teachers. (2002). *Principles for professional development.* Washington DC: Author.

Antoniou, P., & Kyriakides, L. (2013). A dynamic integrated approach to teacher professional development: Impact and sustainability of the effects on improving teacher behavior and student outcomes. *Teaching and Teacher Education, 29,* 1–12.

Association for Supervision and Curriculum Design. (2002). *Every child reading: A professional development guide.* Retrieved from http://www.eric.ed.gov:80/ERICWebPortal/search/detailmini.jsp?_nfpb=true&_&ERICExtSearch_SearchValue_0=ED451498&ERICExtSearch_SearchType_0=no&accno=ED451498

Ball, D. L., & Cohen, D. K. (1996). Reform by the book: What is—or might be—the role of curriculum materials in teacher learning and instructional reform? *Educational Researcher, 25*(9), 6–8.

Ball, D. L., & Cohen, D. K. (1999). Developing practice, developing practitioners. In G. Skykes & L. Darling-Hammond (Eds.), *Teaching as the learning profession: Handbook of policy and practice* (pp. 3–32). San Francisco, CA: Jossey-Bass.

Banilower, E. R., Heck, D. J., & Weiss, I. R. (2007). Can professional development make the vision of the standards a reality? The impact of the National Science Foundation's local systemic change through teacher enhancement initiative. *Journal of Research in Science Teaching, 44*(3), 375–395.

Borko, H. (2004). Professional development and teacher learning: Mapping the terrain. *Educational Researcher, 33*(8), 3–15.

Bransford, J. D., Brown, A. L., & Cocking, R. R. (2000). *How people learn: Brain, mind, experience and school.* Washington, DC: National Academy Press.

Brunn, P. (2010). *The lesson planning handbook: Essential strategies that inspire student thinking and learning.* New York, NY: Scholastic.

Buczynski, S., & Hansen, C. B. (2010). Impact of professional development on teacher practice: Uncovering connections. *Teaching and Teacher Education, 26,* 599–607.

Buysse, V., Castro, D. C., & Peisner-Feinberg, E. (2010). Effects of a professional development program on classroom practices and outcomes for Latino dual language learners. *Early Childhood Research Quarterly, 25*(2), 194–206.

Carpenter, T., Feneman, E., Peterson, P., Chiang, C., & Loef, M. (1989). Using knowledge of children's mathematical thinking in classroom teaching: An experimental study. *American Educational Research Journal, 26*(4), 499–531.

Center for the Collaborative Classroom. (2015). *Making meaning.* Emeryville, CA: Author.

Center for the Collaborative Classroom. (2018). *Caring school community.* Alameda, CA.

Cochran-Smith, M., & Lytle, S. (1993). *Inside/outside: Teacher research and knowledge.* New York, NY: Teachers College Press.

Cochran-Smith, M., & Lytle, S. L. (2001). Beyond certainty: Taking an inquiry stance. In A. Lieberman & L. Miller (Eds.), *Teachers caught in the action: Professional development that matters* (pp. 45–58). New York, NY: Teachers College Press

Costa, A. L., & Kallick, B. (2008). *Learning and leading with habits of mind: 16 essential characteristics for success.* Alexandria, VA: Association for Supervision and Curriculum Development.

Cuban, L. (2013). *Inside the black box of classroom practice.* Cambridge, MA: Harvard Education Press.

Dana, N. F., & Yendol-Hoppey, D. (2008). *The reflective educators guide to professional development.* Thousand Oaks, CA: Corwin.

Dana, N. F., & Yendol-Hoppey, D. (2009). *The reflective educator's guide to classroom research, 2nd Ed.* Thousand Oaks, CA: Corwin.

Dana, N. F., & Yendol-Hoppey, D. (2015). *The PLC book.* Thousand Oaks, CA: Corwin.

Darling-Hammond. (1996). The quiet revolution: Rethinking teacher development. *Educational Leadership, 43*(6), 4–10.

Darling-Hammond, L., Hyler, M. E., Gardner, M. (2017). *Effective teacher professional development.* Palo Alto, CA: Learning Policy Institute.

Darling-Hammond, L., & McLaughlin, M. (1995). Policies that support professional development in an era of reform. *Phi Delta Kappan, 76*(8), 597–604.

Darling-Hammond, L., Wei, R. C., Andree, A., Richardson, N., & Orphanos, S. (2009). State of the profession: Study measures status of professional development. *Journal of Staff Development, 30*(2), 42–50.

Davis, A.W., & Kappler-Hewitt, K. (2013). Australia's campfires, caves and watering holes. *Learning and Leading with Technology, 40*(8), 24–26.

Desimone, L. M. (2009). Improving impact studies of teachers' professional development toward better conceptualizations and measures. *Educational Researcher, 38*(3), 181–199.

Desimone, L. M., Porter, A. C., Garet, M. S., Yoon, K. S., & Birman, B. F. (2002). Effects of professional development on teachers' instruction: Results from a three-year longitudinal study. *Educational Evaluation and Policy Analysis, 24*(2), 81–112.

Dewey, J. (1933). *Democracy and education.* New York, NY: Free Company.

Doppelt, Y., Schunn, C. D., Silk, E. M., Mehalik, M. M., Reynolds, B., & Ward, E. (2009). Evaluating the impact of facilitated learning community approach to professional development on teacher practice and student achievement. *Research in Science and Technological Education, 27*(3), 339–354.

Drago-Severson, E. (2009). *Leading adult learning: Supporting adult development in our schools.* Thousand Oaks, CA: Corwin.

Duffy, G. G., Roehler, L. R., Meloth, M. S., Vavrus, L. G., Book, C., Putnam, J., & Wesselman, R. (1986). The relationship between explicit verbal explanations during reading skill instruction and student awareness and achievement: A study of reading teacher effects. *Reading Research Quarterly, 21*(3), 237–252.

DuFour, R., DuFour, R., Eaker, R., Many, T., & Mattos, M. (2016). *Learning by doing: A handbook for professional learning communities at work* (3rd ed.). Bloomington, IN: Solution Tree Press.

DuFour, R., Eaker, R., & DuFour, R. (Eds.). (2005). *On common ground: The power of professional learning communities.* Bloomington, IN: Solution Tree.

Earley, P., & Porritt, V. (2013). Evaluating the impact of professional development: The need for a student-focused approach. *Professional Development in Education, 40*(1), 112–129.

Easton, L. B. (2008). From professional development to professional learning. *Phi Delta Kappan, 79*(10), 755–759.

Elmore, R. (2004). *School reform from the inside out.* Cambridge, MA: Harvard University Press.

Firestone, W. A., Mangin, M. M., Martinez, M., & Polovsky, T. (2005). Leading coherent professional development: A comparison of three districts. *Educational Administration Quarterly, 41*(3), 413–448.

Fogarty, R., & Pete, B. (2007). *From staff room to classroom.* Thousand Oaks, CA: Corwin.

Fraser, C., Kennedy, A., Reid, L., & Mckinney, S. (2007). Teachers' continuing professional development: Contested concepts, understandings and models. *Professional Development in Education, 33*(2), 153–169.

Fullan, M. (1982). *The meaning of educational change.* New York, NY: Teachers College Press.

Fullan, M. (1992). Visions that bind. *Educational Leadership, 49*(5), 19–20.

Fullan, M. (2005). *Leadership and sustainability: System thinkers in action.* Thousand Oaks, CA: Corwin.

Fullan, M. (2007). Change the terms for teacher learning. *Journal of Staff Development, 28*(3), 35–36.

Fullan, M., Hord, S. M., & von Frank, V. (2015). *Reach the highest standard in professional learning: Implementation.* Thousand Oaks, CA: Corwin.

Gallagher, H. A. (2016). *Professional development to support instructional improvement: Lessons from research.* Menlo Park, CA: SRI International.

Gallagher, H. A., Woodworth, K. R., & Arshan, N. L. (2017). Impact of the National Writing Project's College-Ready Writers Program in high-need rural districts. *Journal of Research on Educational Effectiveness,* 1–26.

Garet, M. S., Porter, A. C., Desimone, L., Birman, B. F., & Yoon, K. S. (2001). What makes professional development effective? Results from a national sample of teachers. *American Educational Research Journal, 38*(4), 915–945.

Goodlad, J., & Klein, F. (1970). *Looking behind the classroom door.* Worthington, OH: Charles A. Jones.

Greenleaf, C. L., Litman, C., Hanson, T. L., Rosen, R., Boscardin, C. K., Herman, J., … Jones, B. (2011). Integrating literacy and science in biology: Teaching and learning impacts of reading apprenticeship professional development. *American Educational Research Journal, 48,* 647–717.

Gulamhussein, A. (2013). Teaching the teachers: Effective professional development in an era of high stakes accountability. *Center for Public Education.* Retrieved from http://www.centerforpubliceducation.org/teachingtheteachers

Guskey, T. R. (2000). *Evaluating professional development.* Thousand Oaks, CA: Corwin.

Guskey, T. R. (2001). The backward approach. *Journal of Staff Development, 22*(3), 60.

Guskey, T. R. (2002). Does it make a difference? Evaluating professional development. *Educational Leadership, 59*(6), 45–51.

Guskey, T. R., & Sparks, D. (1996). Exploring the relationship between staff developments and improvements in student learning. *Journal of Staff Development, 17*(4), 34–38.

Guskey, T. R., & Yoon, K. (2009). What works in professional development. *Phi Delta Kappan, 90*(7), 495–500

Harwell, M., D'Amico, L., Stein, M., & Gatti, G. (2000). *Research contract #RC-96-137002 with OERI.* University of Pittsburgh. Pittsburgh, PA: Learning Research and Development Center.

Hattie, J. (2009). *Visible learning.* London, UK: Routledge.

Hayes, L. F. (2008). Principal as facilitator of learning: Professional development and school reform in the new millenium. Lecture conducted from the University of Florida, United States.

Heller, J. I., Daehler, K. R., Wong, N., Shinohara, M., & Miratrix, L. W. (2012). Differential effects of three professional development models on teacher knowledge and student achievement in elementary science. *Journal of Research in Science Teaching, 49*(3), 333–362.

Hill, H. C. (2004). Professional development standards and practices in elementary school mathematics. *The Elementary School Journal, 104*(3), 215–231.

Hirsch, S. (2017). Make the connection between Learning Forward's standards and ESSA. *The Learning Professional, 38*(4).

Hirsch, S. (2018). Focus professional learning communities on curriculum. *Learning Forward PD Watch.* Retrieved from http://blogs.edweek.org/edweek/learning_forwards_pd_watch/2018/01/focus_professional_learning_communities_on_curriculum.html.

Hoban, G. (2002). *Teacher learning for educational change: A systems thinking approach.* Buckingham, UK: Open University Press.

Hoerr, T. (1996). Collegiality: A new way to define instructional leadership. *Phi Delta Kappan, 77*(5), 380–381.

Isaacson, N., & Bamburg, J. (1992). Can schools become learning organizations? *Educational Leadership, 50*(3), 42–44.

Johnson, C. C., & Fargo, J. D. (2010). Urban school reform enabled by transformative professional development: Impact on teacher change and student learning of science. *Urban Education, 45*(1), 4–29.

Johnson, C. C., & Fargo, J. D. (2014). A study of the impact of transformative professional development on Hispanic student performance on state mandated assessments of science in elementary school. *Journal of Elementary Science Teacher Education, 25*(7), 845–859.

Joyce, B. (1993). The link is there, but where do we go from here? *Journal of Staff Development, 14*(3), 10–12.

Joyce, B., & Showers, B. (2002). *Student achievement through staff development.* Alexandria, VA: Association for Supervision and Curriculum Development.

Joyce, B., Showers, B., & Rolheiser-Bennett, C. (1987). Staff development and student learning: A synthesis of research on models of teaching. *Educational Leadership,* 11–23.

Keene, E. O., & Zimmerman, S. (2007). *Mosaic of thought: The power of comprehension strategy instruction.* Portsmouth, NH: Heinemann.

Kennedy, M. (1998). *Form and substance in in-service teacher education* (Research Monograph No. 13). Madison, WI: National Institute for Science Education.

Kennedy, M. (2016). How does professional development improve teaching? *Review of Educational Research, 86*(4), 945–980.

Killion, J. (2002). *Assessing impact: Evaluating staff development.* Oxford, OH: National Staff Development Council.

Killion, J. (2006). Evaluating the impact of professional development in eight steps. *The Evaluation Exchange, XI*(4).

Kim, J. S., Olson, C. B., Scarcella, R., Kraner, J., Pearson, M., van Dyk, D., Collins, P., & Land, R. E. (2011). A randomized experiment of a cognitive strategies approach to text-based analytical writing for mainstream Latino English language learnings in grades 6 to 12. *Journal of Research on Educational Effectiveness, 4*(3), 231–263.

King, F. (2013). Evaluating the impact of teacher professional development: An evidence based framework. *Professional Development in Education, 40*(1), 89–111.

Kleickmann, T., Trobst, S., Jonen, A., Vehmeyer, J., & Moller, K. (2016). The effects of expert scaffolding in elementary science professional development on teachers' beliefs and motivations, instructional practices, and student achievement. *Journal of Educational Psychology, 108*(1), 21–42.

Knight, J. (2004). Instructional coaching. *StrateNotes, 1*(3): 1–5. Lawrence: University of Kansas, Center for Research on Learning. Retrieved from www.instructionalcoach.org/nov_stratenotes.pdf.

Knight, J. (2007). *Instructional coaching: A partnership approach to improving instruction.* Thousand Oaks, CA: Corwin.

Knight, J. (2011). *Unmistakable impact: A partnership approach for dramatically improving instruction.* Thousand Oaks, CA: Corwin.

Knowles, M. (1973). *The adult learner: A neglected species.* Houston, TX: Gulf Professional.

Kouzes, J., & Posner, B. (1996). Seven lessons for leading the voyage to the future. In F. Hesselbein, M. Goldsmith, & R. Beckhard (Eds.), *The leader of the future.* San Francisco, CA: Jossey-Bass.

Kreider, H., & Bouffard, S. (2006). Questions and answers: A conversation with Thomas R. Guskey. *The Evaluation Exchange, XI*(4).

Landry, S. H., Anthony, J. L., Swank, P. R., & Monseque-Bailey, P. (2009). Effectiveness of comprehensive professional development for teachers of at-risk preschoolers. *Journal of Educational Psychology, 101*(2), 448–465.

Learning Forward. (2011). *Standards for professional learning.* Oxford, OH: Author.

Learning Forward. (2014). Evaluating professional learning: Measuring educator and student outcomes. *Transform Professional Learning* Brief. Retrieved from https://learningforward.org/publications/transform/2014/3/evaluating-professional-learning

Lieberman, A., & Miller, L. (2008). *Teachers in professional communities: Improving teaching and learning.* New York, NY: Teachers College Press.

Little, J. W., Gerritz, W. H., Stern, D. S., Guthrie, J. W., Kirst, M. W., & Marsh, D. D. (1987). *Staff development in California: Public and personal investments, program patterns, and policy choices.* San Francisco, CA: Policy Analysis for California Education (PACE) and Far West Laboratory for Education Research and Development (Policy Paper # PC87-12-15, CPEC).

Louis, K., & Kruse, S. (1995). *Professionalism and community: Perspectives on reforming urban schools.* Thousand Oaks, CA: Corwin.

McCutchen, D., Abbott, R. D., Green, L. B., Beretvas, S., Cox, S., Potter, N. S., … Gray, A. L. (2002). Beginning literacy: Links among teacher knowledge, teacher practice, and student learning. *Journal of Learning Disabilities, 35*(1), 69–86.

McGill-Franzen, A., Allington, R., Yokoi, L., & Brooks, G. (1999). Putting books in the classroom seems necessary but not sufficient. *The Journal of Educational Research, 93*(2), 67–74.

McGowan, G. (2004). *Teaching at risk: A call to action.* New York, NY: The Teaching Commission.

McLaughlin, M., & Talbert, J. (2001). *Professional communities and the work of high school teaching.* Chicago, IL: University of Chicago Press.

Medley, D. (1977). *Teacher competence and teacher effectiveness.* Washington, DC: American Association of Colleges of Teacher Education.

Meissel, K., Parr, J. M., & Timperley, H. S. (2016). Can professional development of teachers reduce disparity in student achievement? *Teaching and Teacher Education, 58,* 163–173.

Moen, R. D., & Norman, C. L. (2009). *The history of the PDCA Cycle.* Paper presented at the Seventh Asian Network for Quality Congress, Tokyo, Japan. Retrieved from https://deming.org/uploads/paper/PDSA_History_Ron_Moen.pdf.

Neale, D. C., Smith, D., & Johnson, V. G. (1990). Implementing conceptual change teaching in primary science. *The Elementary School Journal,* 109–131.

Newman, F., & Associates. (1996). *Authentic achievement: Restructuring schools for intellectual quality.* San Francisco, CA: Jossey-Bass.

Newman, F., & Wehlange, G. (1995). *Successful school restructuring.* Madison, WI: Center on Organization and Restructuring Schools.

Penuel, W. R., Fishman, B. J., Yamaguchi, R., & Gallagher, L. P. (2007). What makes professional development effective? Strategies that foster curriculum implementation. *American Educational Research Journal, 44*(4), 921–958.

Romano, T. (2000). *Blending genre, altering style: Writing multigenre papers.* Portsmouth, NH: Boynton/Cook.

Rosemary, C. A., Roskos, K. A., & Landreth, L. K. (2007). *Designing professional development in literacy.* New York, NY: Guilford Press.

Routman, R. (2004). *Writing essentials.* Portsmouth, NH: Heinemann.

Sarason, S. (1990). *The predictable failure of educational reform.* San Francisco, CA: Jossey-Bass.

Schifter, D., Bastable, V., & Russell, S. J. (1999). *Developing mathematical ideas.* Parsippany, NJ: Dale Seymour.

Seago, N., Mumme, J., & Branca, N. (2004). *Learning and teaching linear functions: Video cases for mathematics professional development.* Portsmouth, NH: Heinemann.

Senge, P. M. (1994). *The fifth discipline field book: Strategies and tools for building a learning organization.* New York, NY: Currency, Doubleday.

Sergiovanni, T. (1994). *Building community in schools.* San Francisco, CA: Jossey-Bass.

Shaha, S. H., Lewis, V. K., O'Donnell, T. J., & Brown, D. H. (2004). *Evaluating professional development: An approach to verifying program impact on teachers and students.* Retrieved from http://cleveland.mspnet.org/index.cfm/11156.

Sirotnik, K. (1983). What you see is what you get: Consistency, persistence and mediocrity in classrooms. *Harvard Educational Review, 53*(1), 16–31.

Sloan, H. (1993). Direct instruction in fourth and fifth grade classrooms. *Dissertation Abstracts International, 54*(8), 2837A.

Sparks, D., & Hirsh, S. (1997). *A new vision for staff development.* Alexandria, VA: Association for Supervision and Curriculum Design.

Stigler, J. W. (1999). *The teaching gap: Best ideas from the world's teachers for improving education in the classroom.* New York, NY: Free Press

Taylor, J. A., Getty, S. R., Kowalski, S. M., Wilson, C. D., Carlson, J., & Van Scotter, P. (2015). An efficacy trial of research-based curriculum materials with curriculum-based professional development. *American Educational Research Journal. 52*(5), 984–1017.

The New Teacher Project. (2015). *The mirage: Confronting the hard truth about our quest for teacher development.* Brooklyn, NY: Author. Retrieved from http://tntp.org/assets/documents/TNTP-Mirage_2015.pdf.

Todnem, G., & Warner, M. P. (1993). Using ROI to assess staff development efforts. *Journal of Staff Development, 14*(3), 32–34.

Trotter, Y. D. (2006). Adult learning theories: Impacting professional development programs. *Delta Kappa Gamma Bulletin, 72*(2), 8.

U.S. Department of Education. (2010). *A blueprint for reform: The reauthorization of the Elementary and Secondary Education Act.* Alexandria, VA: Education Publications Center.

United States Congress. (2001). No Child Left Behind Act of 2001. Washington, DC.

United States Congress. (2009). American Recovery and Reinvestment Act. Washington, DC.

United States Congress. (2015). Every Student Succeeds Act of 1965, 20 USC §§ 1001-8601. Washington, DC.

Van Keer, H., & Verhaeghe, J. P. (2005). Comparing two teacher development programs for innovating reading comprehension instruction with regard to teachers' experiences and student outcomes. *Teaching and Teacher Education, 21*, 543–562.

Vygotsky, L. (1978). Interaction between learning and development. In M. Cole, V. John-Steiner, S. Scribner, & E. Souberman (Eds.), *Mind and society* (M. Cole, V. John-Steiner, S. Scribner, & E. Souberman, Trans., pp. 79–91). Cambridge, MA: Harvard University Press.

Wei, R. C., Darling-Hammond, L., & Adamson, F. (2010). *Professional development in the United States: Trends and challenges.* Dallas, TX: National Staff Development Council.

Wei, R. C., Darling-Hammond, L., Andree, A., Richardson, N., & Orphanos, S. (2009). *Professional learning in the learning profession: A status report on teacher development in the U.S. and abroad.* Dallas, TX: National Staff Development Council.

Whitney, A. E. (2008). Teacher transformation in the National Writing Project. *Research in the Teaching of English, 43*, 144–187.

Wiener, R., & Pimentel, S. (2017). *Practice what you teach: Connecting curriculum and professional learning in schools.* Washington, DC: Aspen Institute.

Wiggins, G., & McTighe, J. (2005). *Understanding by design, expanded 2nd edition.* Alexandria, VA: Association for Supervision and Curriculum Design.

Yoon, K. S., Duncan, T., Lee, S. W.-Y., Scarloss, B., & Shapley, K. L. (2007). *Reviewing the evidence on how teacher professional development affects student achievement* (Issues and Answers Report, REL 2007-No.33). Institute of Education Sciences, National Center for Education Evaluation and Regional Assistance, Regional Educational Laboratory Southwest. Washington DC: U.S. Department of Education.

Zemelman, S., Daniels, H., & Hyde, A. (2012). *Best practice: Bringing standards to life in America's classrooms.* Portsmouth, NH: Heinemann.

# Index

Figures are indicated by f after the page number.

**CORWIN**

A SAGE Publishing Company

**CORWIN HAS ONE MISSION:** to enhance education through intentional professional learning. We build long-term relationships with our authors, educators, clients, and associations who partner with us to develop and continuously improve the best evidence-based practices that establish and support lifelong learning.

## THE PROFESSIONAL LEARNING ASSOCIATION

Learning Forward is a nonprofit, international membership association of learning educators committed to one vision in K–12 education: Excellent teaching and learning every day. To realize that vision, Learning Forward pursues its mission to build the capacity of leaders to establish and sustain highly effective professional learning. Information about membership, services, and products is available from www.learningforward.org.

# Solutions YOU WANT | Experts YOU TRUST | Results YOU NEED

**EVENTS** > > > **INSTITUTES**

Corwin Institutes provide large regional events where educators collaborate with peers and learn from industry experts. Prepare to be recharged and motivated!

**corwin.com/institutes**

**ON-SITE PD** > > > **ON-SITE PROFESSIONAL LEARNING**

Corwin on-site PD is delivered through high-energy keynotes, practical workshops, and custom coaching services designed to support knowledge development and implementation.

**corwin.com/pd**

> > > **PROFESSIONAL DEVELOPMENT RESOURCE CENTER**

The PD Resource Center provides school and district PD facilitators with the tools and resources needed to deliver effective PD.

**corwin.com/pdrc**

**ONLINE** > > > **ADVANCE**

Designed for K–12 teachers, Advance offers a range of online learning options that can qualify for graduate-level credit and apply toward license renewal.

**corwin.com/advance**

Contact a PD Advisor at **(800) 831-6640** or
visit **www.corwin.com** for more information